MYSELF
A MANDARIN
Memoirs of a Special Magistrate

Austin Coates

D0924818

HONG KONG OXFORD NEW YORK
OXFORD UNIVERSITY PRESS
1987

Oxford University Press

Oxford New York Toronto
Petaling Jaya Singapore Hong Kong Tokyo
Delhi Bombay Calcutta Madras Karachi
Nairobi Dar es Salaam Cape Town
Melbourne Auckland

and associated companies in
Beirut Berlin Ibadan Nicosia

First published by Frederick Muller Ltd. 1968
First issued, with permission, in Oxford Paperbacks 1987

ISBN 0 19 584199 9

Printed in Hong Kong
Published by Oxford University Press, Warwick House, Hong Kong

CONTENTS

CONTENTS

I

A Mandate Conferred

A FEW HOURS AFTER BEING directed by the British Government to proceed to Hongkong, I received from them a printed notification advising me that I would need a sword.

Never having had any direct dealings with a government, I found this communication surprising. It was early 1949, I was twenty-six, and in London.

News from China indicated that the armies of the National Government were in retreat before the communist forces of Mao Tse-tung, advancing from the north. Peking had long since fallen to the communists. The National Government of President Chiang Kai-shek had shifted the capital of China southward from Nanking to Canton, only eighty miles or so north of Hongkong. The Chinese Red Army was reported to be less than fifty miles from the Yangtse, in central China. Shanghai was not expected to hold out more than a few weeks.

If the communist advance continued with the *élan* it seemed quite suddenly to have gained, in a matter of months the whole of China could be engulfed, and Hongkong might itself be in danger.

Hongkong had already, under attack by the Japanese in 1941, proved itself militarily indefensible. Doubtless, in the event of an attempted take-over by the communists, some kind of token resistance would have to be offered. Persons employed, as I was to be, in a civil capacity, might have to shoulder arms. This was only reasonable.

Still . . . a sword. . . .

The British Government surely did not believe that in Chinese wars the sword was still a military weapon.

Or did they . . . ?

I read a little more of the printed notification.

It then began to appear that the sword and the Chinese civil war were not connected. This, so far as it went, was reassuring. But it also showed that in some curious way two separate centuries had become entangled. The Chinese civil war was taking place in the twentieth century, while the Hongkong Government, who required me to arrive with a sword, was apparently still living in the Victorian era.

The sword, it turned out, was a ceremonial one, to go with an elaborate white uniform, with gold braid, burnished buttons, aiguillettes, and that symbol of Victorian imperialism, a pith helmet—one of those inverted chamber-pot hats, beneath which a century of viceroys, governors, and lesser dignitaries had concealed all signs of individuality as effectively as a grenadier beneath a bearskin.

From the window of my eyrie of a Mayfair apartment, I gazed at the towers of Westminster and the dome of St. Paul's. My appointment to the civil ranks of the Hongkong Government had already taken effect; since midnight I had been drawing a salary. This was my first order from my superiors. Disobedience I had recognized as being inevitable at some stage of my new career; should it begin quite as early as this? I considered the uniform in more detail.

In my 'teens I was a dramatic student, and I have an actor's sense of miscasting. I might get away with a pith helmet. At least it made for anonymity. But not being very tall, I sensed from the outset that I would not be able to buy a sword the right length for me. I wondered. . . . The wisdom of Saint Eloi in advising King Dagobert to have a wooden sword came home to me strangely. Lighter, less likely to get caught between your legs, and easier to shorten if it was too long.

It might be noticeably wooden, however. On further reflexion, I thought of telephoning my father and asking him if he would be kind enough to seek Ivor Novello's views on the matter. Ivor Novello would know all about swords, and a stage property sword might be all in one piece, which would be an advantage, in that what chiefly concerned me was what would happen if one tripped over it and the blade came out. How would one ever get it back?

The vision, however, of two composers on the telephone discussing swords made me realize that this was a subject liable to lead to misunderstandings. Could I not simply arrive in Hongkong without a sword, with the idea at the back of my mind that, if obliged to attend a function at which the wearing of one was obligatory, I could in an extremity be ill on that day, suddenly and at the last moment taken with a seizure, or perhaps internal spasms?

Without noticing it, I had forgotten all about the Chinese civil war and the dangers, and had become engrossed in a small and comparatively ridiculous local Hongkong problem, almost as if China did not exist. As I was in due course to discover, this is one of Hongkong's most peculiar, and somehow endearing, characteristics. It is separated from China, not by distance, but in time and in mental climate.

When Europeans first settled there, in 1841, Hongkong was a steep, gaunt, scrub-covered rock with only a few hundred Chinese villagers living on it. As a great port and city, it developed from its own special Victorian origins.

China, by contrast, belongs in its own thousands of years of history, stemming from another time, and responsive to other stimuli.

Thus while, on the other side of the border, a civil war of world importance might rage, people in Hongkong were able to pursue their own small personal wars, undeterred by greater events. To anyone interested in these greater events, life in Hongkong was lived in two dimensions: a large dimension, in which the individual was, like Hongkong itself, a dot; and a small dimension, in which ridiculously small local matters seemed very important.

Though I had never been as far east as China, I was not at this time a newcomer to the Orient, having travelled extensively in India, and a fair amount in Burma and South-East Asia. These earlier journeys, however, had been made strictly as a private individual. To return to the Orient as a government official was a new experience, and it seemed to me to be rather unnecessarily encumbered with problems.

On page two of the printed notification there was another disturbing injunction. As I was already aware, I was to be on probation for three years. But before the end of this period, and before I could be confirmed in my appointment, I would have to pass an examination in law.

I knew nothing about law. I had never been inside a law court in any country. I found it difficult to grasp a legal point, or understand the implications of a law. Furthermore, it would be useless to give me instruction. I knew in advance that, as with mathematics, it was a subject I would never be able to understand, and in which I would certainly never succeed in passing an examination.

For a moment I thought of telephoning the Colonial Office, and telling them I had changed my mind about the job. But with a week in which to think it over, I finally settled for the line of least resistance, made my farewells, and sailed for Hongkong.

Feeling small and unworthy, I arrived without a sword, while looming somewhere ahead of me lay the insuperable problem of the law examination.

A few days earlier, Shanghai had fallen, and communist forces had crossed the Yangtse; the rout of the Kuomintang had begun. Canton was still nominally the capital of China, but many of the leaders had left; and already there were rumours of what eventually took place, the evacuation to Taiwan.

Hongkong presented an extraordinary spectacle. The city of Victoria, on the island of Hongkong, and its sister city Kowloon, on the mainland side of the harbour, were at that time geared to provide reasonable accommodation for a population of about 700,000. Since the end of the Second World War the population had topped the million mark, and the place was thus technically already overcrowded when the communist *putsch* began. In the past few weeks, about half a million refugees had poured in from China by air, by train, by steamer and junk, and on foot; and as the months passed, well over another half-million arrived. By early 1950 the population stood at the alarming figure of 2,350,000.

It really seemed as if half Shanghai had descended upon the place, together with all the gold bars in China. Money was flying about at such a rate it was a miracle the Hongkong dollar maintained its purchasing power. Apartment blocks, shops and houses, many of them illegal and sub-standard, were going up at staggering speed, but still not fast enough. All over the rocky hillsides near the urban area, tens of thousands of ramshackle little huts were sprouting day and night, built of packing cases, sacks, kerosene tins, linoleum, worn-out rubber tyres, anything anyone could lay their hands on, tied together with bits of wire, and even with rice straw.

In small agricultural valleys concealed among the low hills of Kowloon peninsula, entire shanty towns were going up in a matter of days. In the streets—grim reminder that the adage is not always true about Chinese civil wars being fought more by compradores than with gunpowder—hundreds of maimed and wounded Nationalist soldiers, who had somehow managed to beg their way south, hobbled or lay about begging alms, sleeping at night where they lay by day, many of them unable to speak Cantonese (the local language), utterly uncared-for, futureless and helpless. From the point of view of orderly government, it was a situation verging on the chaotic.

Nowhere, as I quickly discovered, was the state of crisis more apparent than in the offices of government, most of which were severely understaffed to meet the extraordinary conditions prevailing. It being no time for any ceremonial involving swords and pith helmets, no edict was issued concerning my malfeasance in having come without them. With a hasty injunction to do the best I could about studying law in my spare time, I was set at a desk in the Secretariat, faced by a mountain of files, and told to get on with it.

In the autumn of 1949 Canton fell, the last of the Nationalists escaped to Taiwan and elsewhere, and a few days later contingents of the Chinese Red Army reached the Hongkong border.

The colony had been heavily reinforced, but in the event the troops were not used. Evidently by predetermined deci-

6

sion, the communist advance halted at the border, which was then virtually sealed. It was no longer feasible to go in and out of China, as many of us had till then. Air communications with China, formerly excellent, came to a stop, as did river steamer services to Canton and the Pearl River districts. Trains were no longer allowed to run through from Kowloon to Canton, as they once had; at the frontier it became necessary to de-train, walk across, and take another train the other side.

But in reality, the unexpected happened. Hongkong's relations with the Kuomintang, ever since the '20s, had been a long series of harassments and interference in Hongkong's internal affairs. Far from harassing the colony, the new government in the main left it alone, and did it at least one notable service: it stamped out the piracy which had been endemic for centuries in the waters around Hongkong. For the first time since 1364 there was security of travel in the waters. The river steamers plying between Hongkong and Macao took down their barbed wire and machine guns round the captain's bridge; and it was no longer necessary for night passengers, as a protection for themselves and their valuables, to be locked into their cabins by the huge chains which used to encircle the cabin sections of the ships. Hongkong settled down to seventeen unprecedented years of tranquillity in its relations with China.

Tranquillity induced, in the earlier years at least, by relations being almost non-existent. Indeed, never was Hongkong's separateness from China, and from events there, more manifest. Genuine news from China, as opposed to the happy talk and happy song pealing forth day and night from China's radio stations, was scanty and unreliable. Nor, extraordinary as it may seem, were

7

Hongkong people particularly interested in China news; they had their own local problems and anxieties.

Those years in the life of Hongkong are an epic, of which the place itself, transformed since 1949, is testimony. The refugee squatters posed alarming hazards, particularly in respect of epidemics and fire. But at first it was not certain whether they would remain in the colony. In 1950 more than 200,000 of them returned to China. Only in 1951, when a second exodus from China began, steadier and more gradual this time, did it become clear that they were to be with us for the foreseeable future. The Hongkong Government then embarked on an immense development in schools, hospitals, clinics, all the amenities of urban life, and above all, on the largest and most ambitious housing scheme ever undertaken by any government anywhere, and which Singapore, on a smaller scale, later copied.

On first arrival, I found Chinese people extremely difficult to get on with. By contrast with my friends in India, Burma and Malaya, their almost blinkered concentration on their own personal affairs, their seeming ignorance of, and lack of interest in, anything from the non-Chinese world, and their incessant preoccupation with money, around which the most minute details of life revolved—to a degree which my other Asian friends would have called absurd—made the Chinese seem to me to be as hard as the granite of Hongkong itself.

But there was nothing else for it: if I was to stay for three years in Hongkong and be anything other than miserable, I somehow had to get to know them; and I therefore plunged almost ruthlessly into Chinese society, trying never to miss a social opening.

It was a rewarding experience, leading to the formation

8

of many close friendships; and my initial attitude to Chinese people as a whole changed greatly. But even after three years of concentrated endeavour to understand what was going on around me in the Chinese homes I visited and the company I kept, I still found myself being disconcerted by people's reactions to things, so utterly at variance with the reactions of other races. Faced with a tragedy, a man would laugh, everyone would laugh. Overcome with grief, a woman would not weep, but lose her temper; she might weep next day. The entire reactionary basis of the Chinese people, and their mode of thinking which stemmed from it, seemed to me more akin to the reactions and thoughts of another planet than of another race.

To anyone trying to understand other races in this world, the Chinese surely pose the greatest challenge; and they too have their own difficulties in trying to understand the rest of us. For my own part, I found the pursuit of understanding them was like a game in which I was always a loser. In everything to do with my Chinese friends and acquaintances, I was invariably either a bar late, or else playing in the wrong key.

In the Secretariat, meanwhile, the mountain of files rose till it had to be rearranged as a wall of files, behind which I eventually disappeared. People had to come quite a long way into my office before finding out whether I was there or not.

Meanwhile, too, the months were narrowing to the three-year point when the government would have to decide whether or not to confirm my appointment.

In the matter of not having a sword, I seemed reasonably safe. But every now and then ugly rumblings were heard from the personnel department, complaining about the number of young officers who had not taken their law examinations. Then, one day in my third year, the blow fell.

Laid on my desk was a memorandum, instructing me to divide all urgent work between three of my colleagues, and report the following Monday morning at the Attorney-General's Chambers to complete my law studies.

I still knew nothing about law. I had still never been inside a law court. And needless to say, I had never looked at any of the law books I was supposed to have studied. There had been far too many more interesting things to do. Moreover, what I had now seen of law in the course of my work had confirmed me in the view that, though I might study it for ten years, I could never pass a law examination.

Due to the fact that the Medical Department, like everyone else, was severely overworked, there was a government ruling that an officer might be absent from work on grounds of ill-health for two days, without presenting a doctor's certificate. I had had my eye on this convenient arrangement for some time, wondering whether one day it might come in handy.

That Monday morning, when I was due to report to the Attorney-General, suddenly and at the last moment I had a severe attack of internal spasms, telephoned the Secretariat and others who would need to know, and remained for the permitted two days incommunicado. On Wednesday, when I re-appeared at the Secretariat, concern was expressed and inquiries made about my health. I explained I was feeling much better.

Someone rang up the Attorney-General. At the other end there was a long explanation, at the conclusion of which the officer put the 'phone down. It was most unfortunate, he explained to me. He expressed the Secretariat's formal regrets, but the Attorney-General was so overwhelmed with work that he could not offer me another date.

It was indeed unfortunate, but there it was. Nothing could be done. The three-year point arrived, and my appointment was confirmed.

Six months later, feeling considerably more secure than when I first set out from London, I went on leave to Europe. Towards the end of this period I received a letter from the Hongkong Secretariat, informing me that, on my return, I was to be assigned to the district.

Hongkong is so famous as a port and city that one is apt to forget it has a district. Actually, in those days, the greater part of the colony was rural. One hour by launch or car from the hub of the city, and you could find yourself, if you knew where to go, in a Chinese countryside not fundamentally changed from what it was a thousand years ago. It was a countryside I had travelled in widely, and in which I had an entertaining circle of Chinese acquaintances, ranging from retired bandits to the abbots of Buddhist monasteries concealed amid the more remote and secret hills.

Hongkong was acquired from China in three stages. In 1842 the island of Hongkong and its immediately adjacent islets were ceded to Britain in perpetuity. In 1860 the peninsula of Kowloon, jutting into the harbour from the Chinese mainland, was similarly acquired. This consisted of three square miles of low, rocky hillocks with a few small villages. It has since been extended by reclamation to about five square miles, and is now the site of a soaring and glittering city, the most densely populated area on the surface of the globe.

Finally, in 1898, Britain acquired, on a 99-year lease from China, an area of about 350 square miles, consisting mainly of Kowloon's hinterland. This was a grandly rugged area of grass-covered mountains and sharply-incised valleys, stretching some twenty miles inland. Also included in the lease were about seventy islands scattered around Hongkong, most of them mountainous and, at that time, sparsely inhabited. The islands varied in size from mere pinnacles of rock to one island larger than Hongkong itself.

The New Territories, as the leased area came to be called, had since 1947 been divided into three districts. Two of these, situated beyond the mountains visible from Hongkong harbour, were mainland districts. The Southern District, to which I was appointed, consisted of all that part of the mainland visible from Hongkong harbour, together with all the islands. Much of the district's mainland section was already urban, and becoming industrial. The boundary with ceded Kowloon—Boundary Street—was irretrievably lost in a maze of streets and buildings.

The urban area being the natural geographic centre of the Southern District, the office was in the heart of Kowloon; and I was permitted to continue living in the city. The day after my return, I crossed over to Kowloon to my new office, distinguishable from other city offices by the number of village people coming in and out, or congregated at the doors—people of a kind seldom seen in other parts of town.

The sight gave me a foretaste of what lay ahead. Just as the office was situated in the heart of the city without having anything to do with the city, so would it be with me. I might live and move about in the city, look like a city-dweller, be seen in buses and taxis. From the instant of passing through that office door, I would in effect cease to be in the city, though still visible to those around me. I would belong out beyond, among the hills and islands, in yet another mental climate—a third one.

Not exactly China, not exactly Hongkong, this third mental climate was older in its ways of thought, unchanged by the Chinese politics of fifty years, or by the Hongkong sophistications of a century. It was a separate climate, in which emperors were not unknown, since it lived in a corridor of time devolving directly from the distant past. Even the title of my appointment—Li Man Fu—was centuries old, an archaic imperial title. It was a job which would demand a complete change of thought and attitude after the Secretariat, occupied as I had been there with the doings of the modern world. Yet in this older world, bypassed by time, might I not find the roots—perhaps even the soul—of the people who, met with in the city, held in their hearts something that everlastingly eluded me?

Mentally saying goodbye to Hongkong, I crossed the threshold of that door.

It was a busy office, hierarchically arranged down both sides of a long passage. Beginning with the lavatory (next to the front door) and the tea-brewing room, one passed in succession the permit clerks, the land clerks, the correspondence clerks, the finance clerks, the land demarcators, the typists, the interpreters and (all the time mounting in exaltation) the land officers, before reaching, at the far end, the most exalted office of all—my own.

My arrival, I noticed, caused a reaction. Noisy conversations became quieter. Rough and rapid movements grew more restrained. Eyes fixed on papers rose watchfully. In the Secretariat I had been a mere number. Here, it seemed, I was a personage.

I entered my own office and sat down. Before me on the glass-topped desk was a long blue envelope bearing the crown and seal of the Office of the Governor, and addressed to me. I opened it, and drew forth a heavy piece of blue vellum. At the top of it were the Royal Arms, at the bottom the Governor's signature and the great red seal of the colony. I felt unaccountably nervous. It was a proclamation of some kind, and it appeared to be addressed to me. My name was staring at me out of the middle of it. Had I done something wrong? Uneasily I began to read.

"I, Alexander William George Herder Grantham, Knight Grand Cross of the Most Distinguished Order of Saint Michael and Saint George, Governor and Commander-in-Chief of the Crown Colony of Hong Kong and Its Dependencies, and Vice-Admiral of the same, do by these presents and in virtue of the powers invested in me by . . ."

There followed a jumble about sections and sub-sections of some ordinance or other, which I skipped.

". . . appoint you . . ."

There followed my name.

". . . to be from this day and until further notice under the provisions of . . ."

More sections and sub-sections of some other ordinance, which I again skipped.

Appointed? It was odd. I skipped a line or two more . . . and shuddered.

I was a Magistrate.

Simply by the signature and the great red seal. There was no arguing about it. I already *was* a Magistrate.

When the Emperor of China addressed his officials or his people, his mandates ended with the injunction 'Tremble and obey' The document in my hands did not have to tell me to tremble. I was already doing so. The paper was rattling against the glass.

Examining it more carefully, I noticed moreover that I was not just an ordinary magistrate. It was not as simple as that. I was a Special Magistrate.

With a glazed stare I leaned back and contemplated the ceiling.

Special!

Could any word have been more nicely chosen?

2

The Errant Cow

THE SPECIAL MAGISTRATE—need I explain?—had no court.

The Chief Justice, the Senior Puisne Judge, the Puisne Judge, all the Judges, sat on high benches in full-bottomed wigs with the Royal Arms behind them, in the splendour of teak-panelled courts, with a clerk to announce their comings and goings. No such trappings were apparently considered necessary to signal the dignity of the Special Magistrate. He, as it were, just sat down and was.

He had not been sitting down for more than five minutes when the door opened.

"Can you hear a case, sir?"

"Yes, certainly."

The Chinese clerk-interpreter, lined, benevolent, judicious, circumspect, aged fifty-two or so, years of experience behind him, withdrew slightly to usher in five Chinese peasants, three men, two women, all dressed uniformly in black, the women with black cowls over their heads, their thick brown toes splaying out beyond the width of their clogs, their rough fingers spreading beyond the width of their wrists—those firm, inexpressive hands and feet accustomed to earth and animals, those hands on which the lives of every one of us depend. Without looking at me they sat down at the bidding of the clerk-interpreter in a row of black silence facing my desk.

By an ordinance promulgated when the New Territories were leased from China, it was permissible for litigants to choose whether they would have the magistrate hear their suits according to the common law, or according to Chinese law and custom. The Special Magistrate thus had to be versed in two very different types of law, one English, the other Chinese.

The Special Magistrate knew nothing about the common law, and very little about Chinese law and custom. Faced with an element of choice on the part of litigants, however, he perceived the need to orientate his own views on the matter.

It was difficult to think of anyone in the legal profession, except the Special Magistrate, who would not know a great deal about the common law. A mass of literature existed around it, by means of which fine points could be argued or challenged. On the subject of Chinese law and custom, on the other hand, there was only one known textbook, written by a French Jesuit in the eighteenth century. Only one copy of this book was known to exist, owned by the University of Hongkong. It could not be borrowed, and it was in French.

Having in mind the possibility of appeals—to, say, the Chief Justice—against his decisions, the Special Magistrate saw certain advantages in adhering strictly to Chinese law and custom, a subject about which he must quickly learn as much as possible, building himself into the entrenched position of an expert. Cognate to this was a visit to the University Library, there to find the Jesuit book—though without asking for it—to read as much of it as possible, and then secrete it in a most unlikely place at the top of a twelve-foot ladder, thereafter moving the ladder.

The Special Magistrate, however, as in the space of very

few moments he was about to learn, had entirely misjudged what he was up against.

"Chinese law and custom, I presume?" I said to the clerk-interpreter, with a firm overtone of warning against the unwisdom of replying in the negative.

He nodded. He was a wise old bird. For twenty years he had served in the same district. He must, I judged, know it and its people backwards. The essential incongruity of the situation—that it should be I who was hearing the case, and not he, who must know far more than I ever would—made me wish we could change places. I then reflected that he probably knew nothing about my ignorance of law. A bold showing was indicated. I must not let the side down.

"Well, what's all this about?" I asked.

To my dismay, instead of framing the question politely in Chinese, he almost barked at them:

"All right, what have you come for?"

The man in the centre, not actually looking at me, in the strange way Chinese villagers have when face to face with a foreigner they do not know, replied:

"It's about this cow."

It was an unpromising beginning. Instinctively I glanced from one to the other of the two women, wondering if by any chance the man was referring to one of them. Neither made any sign of being implicated. I collected myself.

"What cow?" I inquired.

"The cow that eats our grass."

"Your grass?"

"Yes, the grass in our village."

"Which village is that?"

He named a place I had not heard of. A query of the interpreter elicited the fact that it was a remote hill village

18

in a roadless area in the eastern mainland part of the district.

"So there's a cow eating grass in your village?"

"Yes."

"Why shouldn't it?"

I began to feel more magisterial. I also began to glimpse an understanding of my interpreter's firm approach to them. They had evidently come before the court with some reason, yet they had a peculiar resistance to explaining what that reason was.

"It won't eat the grass anywhere else," the man answered. "It's in our village every day."

"That's true, Magistrate," put in the man on the right, clearly identifying himself as a village elder. "It passes my door every day."

"You mean it's a cow from another village?" I inquired.

There was a slight stir of relief. I had got the point.

"Yes."

"A cow from another village is eating your grass?"

"Yes."

Groping back through textbooks, my memory came to rest on grazing rights. This was a tricky legal point.

"Is the grass it's eating on private or common land?"

I did not know it, but I had already collided with a buffer. In a Chinese village there is no such legal distinction. I did not catch what the interpreter said, but the man did not understand it.

"It's our grass," he repeated.

This was not good enough. The magistrate was not to be fooled by rustic simplicity.

"Your grass? What do you mean? Is it your own grass, or grass on land owned by the village?"

"It's our village grass."

It was evidently common land. What, I wondered, was the position regarding grazing rights on common land, whether under the common law or under Chinese law and custom? I had by now been a magistrate for just fifteen minutes, and was already at sea.

"Which village does the cow come from?" I asked.

He named another place I had not heard of. The interpreter explained it was another remote hill village about a mile distant from the first.

"Then someone must bring the cow each day to your village."

"No."

"Are you telling me that this cow walks by itself all over the mountains every day to eat grass in your village, and then goes home in the evening all by itself?"

Becoming somewhat irritated, I was relieved to observe that the interpreter's temper was rising in harmony with mine, only rather more so. He had had twenty years of it, after all. The five villagers, now I came to think of it, were facing me with the obstructiveness of five armoured tanks.

The procedure of the court gradually became apparent to me. Its function was not to provide a means whereby complainants might express their grievances. At least, not all at once. The procedure was less explicit, more defensive. Faced with five or six unknown people, it was the magistrate's duty to find out why on earth they were there.

"No, the cow doesn't come by itself," said the man in the centre.

"Then someone must bring it."

"No."

"Who milks the cow?" I demanded.

The interpreter repeated my question angrily before recalling himself to common sense. A tremor of embarrassment at such an odd and faintly improper inquiry passed along the five. The interpreter hastily explained to me that cows are not kept for their milk, but as draught animals. It was stupid of me. I knew quite well that Chinese did not drink cow's milk, but somehow . . . a cow. . . . We were in a mess.

"If the cow doesn't come by itself," I asked, "how does it get there?"

"Get there?" the man replied in a puzzled tone.

"Yes. How does it come from its own village to your village?"

"It doesn't."

"But you've just been telling me it does, every day!"

The temperature was rising. The interpreter was near to shouting at the man. For my own part, I could not recall ever having had my way so completely blocked by a cow.

"It doesn't come every day."

"But you have just said it does!"

"No. Not every day."

"Then it doesn't eat your village grass every day."

"Yes, it does."

"For goodness' sake, Mr. Lo," I expostulated to the interpreter, "what is this man talking about?—Look. Either this cow comes from the other village every day and eats your grass, or it doesn't come from the other village every day. And if it does come from the other village every day, someone must be bringing it."

"No. No one brings it."

"Then it doesn't eat your grass every day!"

"Yes, it does."

Even the villager's temper showed signs of rising by this time. He seemed to have adopted the attitude that it was I who was being stupid, not he.

"Then, for heaven's sake, how does it get home to the other village at night?"

"It doesn't go home to the other village."

"Well, where does it sleep, then? On the mountain?"

Mr. Lo, I was glad to note, was participating full-blast in this battle of intellect. The impatient *hauteur* with which he sniffed 'On the mountain?' would have reduced anyone other than a New Territories villager to shamed silence.

"No," the villager said calmly. "It sleeps in our village."

Mr. Lo sighed and shook his head. I took a deep breath and started again.

"Now, let's get this straight. A cow from another village eats the grass in your village every day, but it sleeps in your village."

"Yes."

"Well, what does the owner of the cow say to that?"

"Nothing."

"Well then, what are you complaining about?"

Dead silence.

"Repeat the question, Mr. Lo."

"What are you complaining about?" the interpreter repeated. He looked very angry. If I had been the villager I would have been terrified. None of the five armoured tanks expressed the slightest reaction.

I leaned back deeply in my chair, and took out a cigar. In moments of stress, nothing is so soothing as a cigar. Mr. Lo was watching me cautiously. I had a slight sense of guilt. There was no Royal Arms behind me. I had no wig or clerk of court. Yet . . .

"Is it considered proper to smoke while hearing cases, Mr. Lo?"

"Most district officers find it a help, sir."

"Good. Can you ask someone to find me a match?"

22

The necessary orders were issued. A box of matches appeared. In ancient China, part of a magistrate's duty was to soothe the people. In the modern world, the more cogent factor seemed to be the soothing of the magistrate. A film of blue smoke went up.

"Now then," I resumed, "do you use the cow in the fields?"

"A little."

The expression he had actually used was a Chinese ambiguity which could mean 'Yes', 'Hardly at all', or 'No'. Mr. Lo, taking his choice, had settled for a middle course.

"A little!" I exclaimed. "What do you mean by that? Do you or do you not use the cow?"

"No."

"Have you ever used it?"

"Yes."

"Did the owner complain?"

"No."

"But he's complaining now."

"Yes."

"He wants the cow back in his own village."

"Yes."

I clenched the desk.

"But when you came in here, you began, if you can remember, by complaining that a cow from another village was eating your grass!"

"Yes. There's no suitable grass in the other village."

It was incomprehensible.

"Who is the owner of the cow?" I asked.

"Her," said the man, using a rough, off-hand word, indicating the woman on his right.

Beneath her black cowl, the half-hidden little face stirred.

23

"Ah!" I said. "Now we're coming along. You are the owner of the cow?"

"Yes."

"Yes, *what*!" the interpreter snapped at her.

"Yes, Magistrate," the woman said demurely.

It was too awful for words. At the very entrance of a woman into the picture, the interpreter's voice had hardened. I did not, of course, know at the time that this was another outcome of my skilled interpreter's experience—that it is hard enough to get sense out of a village man, still worse to get sense out of a village woman, and that a woman litigant or witness, unless dealt with from the outset with the utmost firmness, will set any case in the wildest disorder.

"You are from the other village?" I said.

"Yes, Magistrate."

"And you want the cow back?"

"Yes."

"How did this man start using your cow in the first place? Did you allow him to?"

"Yes."

"And now you've changed your mind?"

"Yes."

"Did you charge him any money for the use of it?"

"No."

"But you want the cow now for use on your own fields?"

"I have no fields, Magistrate."

"Then what do you want it back for?"

"I want it back."

"What d'you want it back *for*?" the interpreter barked at her.

The little face beneath the cowl hardened.

"I want it back."

24

"Is it true," I asked, "that there isn't enough suitable grass in your village to feed the cow?"

"There isn't much."

"There's none," said the man.

"Then would it not be more sensible," I said to the woman, "to continue to allow this man the use of your cow, but charge him for it?"

"I wouldn't pay!" said the man sharply.

There was something in the way he said it. And at this moment, the magistrate, lulled by the cigar, became subject to a brainwave.

"You say you come from the other village?" I asked the woman.

"Yes."

"Where do you actually live?"

"In *his* village," she said, nodding at the man, and using the same off-hand expression he had used about her.

"Mr. Lo, there is a relationship of some sort between these two people. Can you find out what it is?"

The interpreter asked a rapid question. There was a scowling silence, then a word from the man. They were husband and wife.

"Ah!" I said, and addressing the wife, "The position is that you want to go back to your village, and you want to take your cow with you. Is that it?"

"Yes, Magistrate."

We had arrived. It was a divorce case.

By this time, the magistrate felt he had had about enough. He also felt it was about time the staff started exerting themselves on his behalf.

For this was what lay behind the manner in which the case had been presented to me—neat, as it were. It was a new officer's first day, and the staff were unsure of themselves, waiting to find out what methods the new officer would use, and also—perhaps more salient—how much he knew. It was almost certainly with this latter point in mind that the clerk-interpreter had introduced the case without making any prior inquiries of his own, leaving me to make all my own mistakes.

The district, with its population of some 250,000, and its large and rapidly expanding industrial zones, was a hectically busy place. If the district officer was to deal personally with every case from the start, the work of the office would rapidly come to a standstill.

"Mr. Lo, will you please take these people out to your office, disentangle the facts, and when you are able to explain the thing to me clearly, bring them back, and we'll go into it."

Thereafter, this became the procedure. It did not eliminate the absurd misunderstandings of which my own ignorance was a main cause; but it did at least minimize them.

About an hour later, Mr. Lo returned with the group, and the case came to make sense. The woman on the man's left—the one who had so far said nothing—was a second wife, married about a year previously. The first wife, who had been married to the man for four years, and had brought the cow with her, complained that the husband was cruel to her, neglecting her in favour of the new wife. She wished to divorce her husband, and return to her own village.

The village elder insisted that the case was nonsense, that the husband was not in the least cruel to the first wife, that on the contrary the woman had a shocking temper, and should learn to be more kind to her husband.

By the degree of the elder's intrusion into the affair,

however, I hazarded an unspoken guess that he had a stake in it. He spoke gravely of the disgrace of divorce, of the pointlessness of the woman returning to her own village. My private conclusion was that he did not much care whether the woman left her husband or not. The elder's moralizing had an un-Chinese ring about it, specially prepared for foreign ears. What he did not wish to see leave the husband was the cow, which the elder was probably using on his own fields.

As for the husband, it was hard to say whether he was more concerned about his wife or the cow. It looked to me like a bit of both, coupled with the fact that his second wife gave him more comfort than his first.

The relations between the husband and the first wife were clearly very bad indeed. They had not looked at each other once. When one spoke of the other, each turned stiffly the other way. The wife was tense, her pride injured. The husband was sour and aggrieved, possibly knowing somewhere he had done his first wife an injury by marrying the second, but far too obstinate ever to admit it.

In general—but I do not think I was aware of it till that moment—I dislike anything in life involving the severance, in anger and unforgiveness, of attachments through the medium of which sympathy and understanding have once flowed. Whether in marriage, friendship or parental relations, such severances seem to me to dishonour life. Basic in the approach to a case of divorce—and I was surprised by the strength of my own conviction—it seemed to me to be the magistrate's duty to struggle to prevent divorce, to restore harmony. But when they are sitting in front of you, with faces like these, how to set about it?

The question I wished answered was the one which could not be asked: whether or not the wife's motive in

27

seeking divorce was that she had a lover. This inadmissible, there remained the factor which had not so far entered into the case—law. Could it not perhaps be used, albeit in a somewhat unlikely way? As a warning rattle.

"Are you your husband's *kit fat*?" I asked the first wife—a *kit fat* is the first wife, a man takes, ranking senior to any other wife he may subsequently take.

"Yes."

"Mr. Lo, I thought that, in Chinese law and custom, there was no such thing as divorce between a husband and his *kit fat*."

"That's long ago, sir. Nowadays, divorce is recognized custom."

My first attempt had failed.

"Have you any children?" I asked the wife.

"Two girls."

It was old Chinese law and custom that, in divorce, boys go to the husband, girls to the wife.

"You realize you will be solely responsible for the girls' upkeep?"

She was silent for a long time. There was always the possibility that a foreign magistrate might not know the old Chinese laws.

"Yes," she said at last.

"Do you think you can feed them? You have already told me you have no fields."

"I shall try my best."

"How will you do it?"

"I don't know."

The elder had craned forward tensely. The husband was scarcely breathing. It inclined me to think there was not a lover. What seemed to be at issue was the cow.

"Don't you think you'd better think it over carefully for

28

a week, and come and see me again? I don't want to give you a divorce, and then find you here a month later, asking for social welfare money for the upkeep of your children. If that happens, the government will blame *me*."

For the first time in the hearing, the woman raised her eyes and looked straight into mine. It had obviously never occurred to her that a magistrate could be in trouble because of her. Unconsciously, I had touched something. In some peculiar way, I had become personally involved in the affair. She was not, as the elder had insisted, a scolding woman. That was not the truth. There was something else to it. But what? She was a nice little woman.

I looked down the line of faces, stern, withdrawn. How to find out the truth from behind such barriers of reticence? Whom to question? What to ask? How to avoid the easy, but unsatisfactory, decision? How to gain access to the right one?

In a Western court, someone would have had to prove cruelty, with witnesses publicizing all kinds of unpleasantness, much of which might be faked. Here, no such thing. There they sat in front of you, awaiting your decision, in an atmosphere of suffering and frayed tempers, waiting for you to help them; and there you were, with no sure facts, no definite evidence, nothing much to go on, but such small corners of truth as they were prepared to show, beyond which lay something else hidden, unidentifiable. . . .

A week later they came again. In the intervening time we had heard quite a number of other cases, and Mr. Lo was beginning to feel more at ease with me. Actually, the staff as a whole had now had time to assess me. What their real verdict was, I would never know, of course; but they seemed to have decided that I needed help. Mr. Lo had done some homework on the divorce case; and as he entered the room, something about his appearance suggested that he had arrived at the root of the problem.

"I didn't realize," he said, "but that second wife, the one who said nothing—she has a son."

"A son? The husband's?"

"Yes. Only a few weeks old."

I leaned back contentedly in my chair.

"Ah! I see! And the first wife only had two daughters."

"That's it."

That was indeed it! And to think I had thought of asking everything else except that! I had, as it were, been mesmerized by the cow.

"Ask the first wife to come in, Mr. Lo. Alone."

She came—'alone' meant with Mr. Lo—and the diagnosis was confirmed. What was closer to the bottom of it than anything else we could find (you never quite got to the bottom of any case) was that she had lost face dreadfully by the birth of the second wife's son. This ascertained, I went all out to reason her back into staying with her husband.

It was then I began to appreciate the wisdom of Mr. Lo's hardness of tone when it was a woman he was questioning. The more understanding of her problem I tried to show, the more impossible she became. Her response to every artifice of reasoning was to put forth yet another demand, which her husband must obey if she was to remain with him. These mounted in number and ferocity till, had we brought wife and husband to written agreement, the result would have read like an armistice between victor and vanquished.

Worse still, I observed that I was alienating Mr. Lo, whose temper, like a balloon of which someone has surreptitiously cut the moorings, was rising independent of the human will it was supposed to serve. Seeing I was on a wrong course, and anxious not to be left behind by the rising balloon, I finally feigned an outburst of temper superior to Mr. Lo's.

"I've had enough of this nonsense!" I said to the wife. "You're darned well going to stay with your husband; and I'm not so sure I don't believe what the village elder says about your being an impossible woman to live with."

She quietened down immediately. I felt remorse.

"Don't worry," I said. "Maybe you'll be the next one to have a son."—A rumour of a smile across her lips showed that this was not beyond the bounds of possibility.—"And you must admit it will be nice for your cow to be able to eat the grass it likes."

At that moment I learned another lesson. The magistrate should never try to be funny. She burst into tears.

The problem now was that we had the facts of the case, but the Special Magistrate was at the end of his resources. How to settle the affair?

"What d'you think we ought to do, Mr. Lo?"

He reflected an instant.

"I should just give them a talking-to, sir."

"A talking-to?" I said, aghast. "What d'you mean? A sort of old-fashioned homily?"

"Yes, I think that would do."

And so, I called them in, and gave them a homily—the first of many, in many different cases. Throughout my years as a magistrate I was never able to reconcile myself to this Chinese method of settling matters. To the end, I always found my own homilies acutely embarrassing, mainly because I could never believe they would settle anything, and they seemed so dreadfully glib.

31

But when, later on, I came to hear cases assisted by other members of the staff, I found that they too agreed with Mr. Lo on the importance of a homily as a means of bringing peace. As one of the staff explained to me, many of the people who were brought to us by their village elders (as had happened in this divorce case) were brought for the express purpose of being given a homily—being told what to do, and how to behave—after which there would be peace, the magistrate's word being law.

In other countries, of course, a magistrate's word is law; but really, only when he is delivering his findings. In this antique Chinese village world, amid the shadows of departed dynasties, there was the difference that the Magistrate's *every* word was law. One had to be very careful what one said.

In this, my first case, therefore, I began by declining to agree to a divorce. Addressing the husband, I told him he had done a very foolish thing in taking a second wife. He should have been more patient. His first wife might very well bear him a son. He had however been impatient, and would have to take the consequences. Instead of having to bear the taunts of one wife, he now had to bear the taunts of two. Instead of having to be fair and patient with one wife, he now had to be fair and patient with two. Let him see that he was. He was the master of his own house. If he were giving a feast in his house, he would not wish to see some guests well provided for, while others did not have enough to eat. It was the same with his wives. As guests are invited to a feast, so had he invited them to his house. As guests must be provided for equally, so must it be with his wives. If he remembered this always, there need be no trouble. And let him never forget that he was the master, which meant that while he had his duties to every person under his roof, it must also be he who gave the orders.

To the first wife, I said I realized she had had a distressing and difficult time. This, however, did not mean that she could disobey her husband, and do what she would. She must always obey her husband. It was good that she had brought her case before me, because she was in distress, and did not know what to do. If she was ever in distress again, she must come at once and tell me about it. She had nothing really to complain of. She was the senior wife; and the little boy born to the second wife would have to call her Mother. Nothing could shake her position in the family, unless she herself was foolish enough to shake it—which I felt sure she would not be, particularly now that she knew she could come at any future time, and ask the court to help her. She was a woman of means, owning her own cow, and being senior wife to a hard-working and well-thought-of farmer. She should be proud of her position.

To the second wife, I said I was very glad to know she had borne a son. She was a fortunate and happy woman, married to a good and sensible man. Her position in the household was that of second wife, bound to obey the orders of the first wife. I was aware from her behaviour in the court, I said, that she had appreciated this from the first day of entering the house. I trusted she would continue to do so. She should guard against boasting about being the mother of her husband's eldest son, as I was sure she would, since boasting about a son brings ill-luck; and the loss of a son would mean ill-luck to the whole family.

The second wife, who had been expressionless throughout, unexpectedly smiled.

"I see you know what I mean about not boasting," I said. "Does your little boy have a girl's name?"

"No, Magistrate," she said, in hasty confusion.

"What do you call him, then?"

She blushed, and did not know where to look.

"We call him Pig," she whispered.

"Very wise," I said. "Then heaven will not take him away from you; and all of you in this united family will have prosperity. Make sure your little boy, when he is old enough, always obeys his Elder Mother. And may there be many more sons among you!"

I went with them to the door, and, holding Mr. Lo beside me, in a friendly European, but highly improper Chinese, way laid my hand beneath the wrist of the senior wife.

"No more nonsense from you," I said, when the others were out of earshot. "But if it's serious, come and see me at once."

She was terrified, and ran away. I felt as if I had made an indecent suggestion.

We never saw them again—not surprising, some might say.

But did it signify success or failure? That, as I was soon to learn, was the most hauntingly worrying of a magistrate's problems—never knowing the full extent of one's own failures. Some of the failures returned quickly enough. But what of those others, of which the only outcome was silence?

In the office they said that, in most cases, silence could be interpreted as success. I was never sure myself. Sometimes—many times, I fear—it was the silence of disappointment at the magistrate's inability to understand.

Because, being a European, one never does *quite* understand. . . .

I walked back slowly towards my desk, and a final incongruity struck me. Before me, between two windows looking out on a small, tree-covered hillock, was a portrait of Her Majesty the Queen. What more simple example of the strangeness of Hongkong could there be than the scene this room had just witnessed? There we had been, beneath the beneficent gaze of our Christian sovereign, quietly engaged in promoting harmony among concubines.

3

Male, Female, and One

THE COW CASE, in which everybody began at the winning post, the magistrate having to pull them firmly backwards till they reached the starter's line, demonstrated a tendency which had long interested and puzzled me: the unusual difficulty Chinese people seemed to have in explaining things, beginning at the beginning.

Though more marked in the rustic, and in the uneducated, it was by no means confined to them. Since my earliest days in Hongkong, I had confronted it again and again in widely differing circumstances. It designated, I had concluded, a mental process, or a quality of the mind itself, which differed from our own in some way peculiarly difficult to analyse.

I had questioned many Chinese friends about it, without receiving any completely convincing answer. Chinese friends, when they know you are interested, will go to infinite pains to explain a point concerning their civilization, often returning to it weeks later, making you realize that, in the interim, they have been trying to think out a means of conveying the idea to a foreign mind.

For this, too, is a problem which China presents more strikingly than any other land. As a foreigner, you are—though it sometimes takes years to become aware of it (and perhaps one never knows its full extent)—daily surrounded by apparently simple things—objects, happenings, manners—the nature of which seems to leave nothing in doubt, the inner significance of which, however, is totally different from anything you would have expected. Time and again, you need a guide to arrive at it.

To take a simple example: in my first weeks in Hongkong, I had to furnish a large room with a great deal of bare wallspace. Ferreting about in antique shops, I found, at a very reasonable price, two sensitively-painted scroll portraits: one of a Manchu official of the last century, wearing his mandarin robes; the other of his wife, wearing a magnificent costume, which I took to be that of a bride. I hung them in my room, to which they gave an atmosphere of sober dignity, fitting to the old-fashioned house with its high ceilings.

The portraits had been hanging there for three months before—quite by chance, and in another person's house—I found out what they were. They were posthumous portraits, commissioned by the relatives of the deceased, and intended to be hung on one day only: the annual feast for the dead, to which none but family members are invited. With embarrassment I recalled the numerous Chinese friends whom I had entertained at home, realizing for the first time the macabre impression my room must have given them. That night the two portraits came down; and the following day I was once more in the antique shops, beginning again.

This is the kind of thing for which, living among Chinese, one has to be prepared. Unexpectedly, a shaft of sunlight illuminates what you had considered a familiar corner of your room, revealing it to be quite other than you expected. Beneath the surface of every day lies a continual struggle to understand the deceptively different realities underlying the visible nature of things.

Returning to Hongkong on the evening of my first day in office, I went round to see my Buddhist friend, Third Brother. He was a business man with a rickety old office magnificently situated, facing the waterfront. It was after office hours, and Third Brother was seated at his desk in the window overlooking the great harbour.

With considerable hilarity on both sides, I explained how that morning a cow had turned into a divorce, after which, in a more serious tone, I asked what, in his opinion, lay at the root of this strangely roundabout mental approach to things. I was convinced, I said, that it was not stupidity; yet this was what it looked like. He smiled cryptically, and did not at once reply.

Then, taking a sheet of paper, he moistened a Chinese writing brush, and on the paper made a single stroke, thus:

丿

"This stroke," he said, "thick at the top, thin at the bottom, is a male stroke, representing the masculine principle."

Near this stroke he made another:

"This second stroke," he went on, "thin at the top, thick at the bottom, is a female stroke, representing the feminine principle. Joining these two principles together, the masculine and the feminine"— 人 —"you have created the character *yan*, meaning mankind.

"Now, here," he continued, making this stroke—near the character *yan*, "we have the character *yat*, meaning the numeral one.

"What happens if, instead of making the character *yat* separate and on its own, we lay it across the upper part of the character *yan*—across the upper part of mankind, you see, where the mind is?"

Across the upper part of the character *yan* he made the horizontal stroke of *yat*, producing this: 大

"Now, what have we created?" he asked me.

"You've made the character *tai*, meaning great," I replied.

"Precisely. And that is the answer to your question. There it is, in one of the simplest characters of the Chinese language, which expresses an idea as old as the race itself, an idea in which we are nursed and brought up. The character *tai* expresses it like a formula: mankind, plus single-mindedness, equals great."

In other words, anyone who wishes to succeed in life must be single-minded in purpose.

I have ever since believed in the validity of Third Brother's explanation. The Chinese people have, to a degree not found among other races, a peculiar single-minded concentration each on his or her own affairs, rendering it unusually difficult for them to appreciate that the whole of their thought at a moment in time, together with the whole of what led up to that thought, has to be transferred from their own mind to that of another, if that thought is to be understood. In time, I came to learn to avoid, in my court, asking certain questions which, though simple and relevant, were likely to prove unanswerable. Was it a fine day when you returned to the village, or was it raining? More likely than not, the answer would be: I have no recollection. Did it take you a long time to reach the village?—I don't remember.

Much of what at first appeared to be obstructionism could be accounted for by remembering this quality of single-mindedness. Questioning a Chinese differs in many ways from questioning a European, who, for example, while travelling by train to London for the first hearing of his own divorce case, might at the same time have noticed that the leaves of the trees were showing the first tints of autumn, that the hat of the woman opposite him was red, and that her little boy had bad manners. Going through a moment of stress, the European might not notice all these things, but there was a high likelihood that he would notice some of them. With a Chinese, the likelihood would lie in the other direction. Unless proved to the contrary, one could safely assume that he had noticed none of them.

The European's mind, the Chinese might say, was diffuse, leading to wastefulness of mental energy, and even to incoherence. The Chinese mind, the European might reply, was so acutely concentrated as to lead to an extreme self-centredness, giving the outward impression of being unsystematic.

Neither would be entirely right. Neither would be entirely wrong.

4

A Public Hearing

AMONG THE FILES in my in-tray was one concerning a dispute over the ownership of some watercress beds on one of the district's larger islands. My predecessor had held a preliminary hearing of the case, and made notes on it, in the course of which he recorded that no one involved had been able to explain a point, which appeared to be of some importance, concerning the exact position of the watercress beds in relation to other fields. He had marked the place down for a visit; but in his last weeks before going on leave, he had not had time to do more than this. In a note of apology to me, he advised a visit as the only means of grasping the facts.

It did not sound a particularly pleasant case, the contestants being an absentee landlord and a cultivator. Having myself seen a good deal of the absentee landlord, however, in various Asian countries, he was a subject on which I held fairly informed views; and it occurred to me that this might be a suitable case to hear in public at the village itself.

I had for some weeks been concerned about the privacy of the Special Magistrate's doings, a privacy rendered unavoidable by the fact that he had no court, and thus had to hear cases in his office, which was not large enough for more than those immediately concerned to be admitted.

Justice, as the old adage went, must not only be done; it must be seen to be done.

The watercress beds were situated somewhere in a sharply indented valley of ricefields, around the sides of which, at the foot of steeply rising mountains, were five small, scattered villages, founded during the Ming dynasty. The rice land was very flat, having around the year 1300 been entirely under the sea. In recent years, the sand beach facing the sea had become one of the colony's most popular swimming places, to which thousands of people poured out of town at weekends by ferry and launch. There were two seaside hotels there, one of which had a large ground-floor restaurant, which would be a suitable spot to use as a makeshift court.

Calling for Mr. Lo, I arranged for a Chinese letter to be sent to the hotel manager, asking that we be allowed to use the restaurant. I then fixed a day for the hearing, which would include an inspection of the watercress beds, and ordered the office launch.

Mr. Lo, I noticed, reacted to this with the first signs of that psychic alienation which, in its advanced stages, led to the rise of the independent balloon. He looked dubious. He said nothing, however; and I shrugged it off. He often looked dubious. Years of listening to people talking in riddles had given him a permanently dubious look when his face was in repose.

His reticence was not, however, shared by my senior land officer, a European of great experience, who had worked in the district for years, and knew it like the back of his hand. Half an hour had not passed before he entered my room.

A burly, jovial fellow with a tremendous sense of humour, he generally burst in all smiles. On this occasion, hc entered with slow gravity. He was much older than myself, and, like Mr. Lo, knew far more about everything than I did. His look of gravity thus bore in it a fatherly air of reprimand. I saw I had committed a misdemeanour of some kind, and was in for a lecture.

"Do I hear you're proposing to hear that Mui case in public?" he inquired.

"Yes, I had thought so," I replied—Mui was the name of the absentee landlord.

"D'you think that's wise?"

"Why should it not be?"

"The communists are pretty interested in this case, you know."

"Really?" I said nonchalantly. "Yes, I suppose they would be."

It had not occurred to me till then, but the case— between an absentee landlord and a cultivator—could well turn out to be a communist agrarian classic.

"They'll be there. We know," he continued with emphatic gravity. "In strength."

"Suppose the case goes in favour of the cultivator?" I inquired, confident of my ability to deal with an absentee landlord.

"H'm!" he sniffed. "In law, the cultivator hasn't a leg to stand on. I know this case. It's a bastard."

This, though I tried not to let him see it, rather took the wind out of my sails. I had envisualized the case as a good local news story, showing that the Hongkong Government helped the underdog, etc.

"Why don't you hear it in here?" he pursued.

"I've made the arrangements now. I don't think we should change them."

His broad shoulders heaved as he turned away. "Well,

you know what you're doing, I suppose." (He was not given to making compliments.) "But if I were you"—he paused at the door— "*I wouldn't!*"

He was, of course, perfectly right, though I was too obstinate to admit it. Though relations between China and Hongkong were tranquil, the colony was treated by Peking as one of the overseas territories in which communism was to be encouraged and, where necessary, financially supported. There was a local communist party, communist newspapers, and the usual arrangements for local subversion.

None of it had been a conspicuous success. Hongkong has its own ways of doing things, and some of them proved difficult to change. At the earlier communist reunions, cocktails were served, there was ballroom dancing, and on one occasion, when a reunion was held directly opposite my apartment in downtown Victoria, the communist chief and his lady entertained to the ebullient strains of the Emperor Waltz.

Such disgraceful goings-on had to be stopped, of course; though even then it did not prove too easy. At one time communist officers sent from China for duty in Hongkong had to be replaced every six months, due to the speed with which they became corrupted by prosperity. All told, Peking had had a trying time endeavouring to lick the Hongkong Communist Party into shape. Like most other organizations in Hongkong, it had a tendency to be frightfully respectable and distressingly bourgeois.

But it had good claws; and one of these was the Chung Chik Kung Wui, milkily translated by the Hongkong Government as the Planters' Association, a small, compact group, formed with the aim of fanning rural discontent, and which was what my senior land officer was referring to

44

in connexion with the case of the watercress beds. Should the case go against the cultivator, he might have to be thrown off his watercress beds—a moment the Wui would probably choose to stage a communist demonstration.

Furthermore, it would not end with a demonstration. In town there were a number of lawyers whose practices included the defence of communist cases, and who were prepared to forsake the Supreme Court for surprisingly long periods, in order to take up small, unremunerative cases such as those coming before my court. Their object then was, by a process of successive appeals, to raise such suits to the highest juridical level, each appeal accompanied by increasingly vociferous outbursts of anti-government propaganda in the communist press.

If the communists really got their teeth into it, this modest dispute concerning three watercress beds, the total size of which was equivalent to a tomato patch in a London back garden, was capable of becoming the subject of hourly bulletins issued by Peking Radio throughout the world in twenty-five languages. My informal, over-the-desk court, in which—in suitable circumstances—cigarettes, and even cigars, were handed round as a means to quiet concentration, reason and civility, was not (as the office staff was aware) quite so obscure as it looked—potentially.

By the time I developed cold feet about the case, however, the letter to the hotel manager had already been despatched; and to alter the arrangements would, I considered, be interpreted by the communists as a sign of weakness.

This was doubly likely due to the attitude of my own staff. Certain atmospheric changes in the office over the ensuing days had indicated to me that the senior land officer was not alone; his opinions were shared by everyone.

Much that went on in the office was known to the communists; this would certainly be known. As with my posthumous portraits, I was once more off on a wrong course.

It took an hour and a half to reach the island from Hongkong. Before our launch even neared the pier, it could be seen from movements around the hotel—about a quarter of a mile away—that people had begun to assemble. In silence, Mr. Lo and I rounded the rocky path leading from the pier to the long and superb sand beach, crescent-shaped, in the centre of which, fronting the nearest of the five villages, was the seaside hotel.

Entering the restaurant, we found waiting for us a crowd of between seventy and eighty villagers, all of them men, with more arriving each minute. It looked as though every able-bodied man in the valley had come. The reception we were given was reserved and disdainful. The villagers had clearly been told to expect the magistrate to be on the landlord's side. They had come cynically prepared to witness injustice done, and, as their numbers suggested, their presence had been organized. It was unpleasant.

Alone and ignored was the absentee landlord, a plump, pasty-faced man, not very tall, wearing a dark brown Chinese long gown.

He was conspicuously urban. His whole appearance suggested secret riches, extravagant parties in obscurely select Chinese-speaking clubs, the maintenance of concubines in separate houses. His fat white hands had observably never handled anything heavier than a safe-deposit key; and the nail of the little finger of his left hand was two inches long. Unless he conducted his case very well, he was a sitting target for our communist friends, several of whom must be somewhere in the group, waiting for their moment.

Standing forth, a few paces in front of the massed body

46

of men, dressed in peasant's black, was the cultivator—a tall, thin, sinewy man with brooding, sullen, worried eyes. His skin was of a wan, lifeless yellow, suggestive of village gambling and opium-smoking, making me wonder for an instant whether he was even, in fact, a cultivator. A glance at his hands showed that he was.

I greeted him coldly with a nod, thereafter turning my attention to the landlord, whom, with a smile and a jest, I invited to accompany me on an inspection of the watercress beds.

Leaving the seaside area, with its garish advertisements, its flags and megaphones silently waiting to relay hell on Sunday, we moved out, on a narrow strip amongst the squared fields, into the rice area, surrounded by its green, treeless mountains.

It was June, the weather hot and bright—blue sky and huge clouds building up for rain, perhaps tomorrow or the day after. A few yards into the rice area, and we were reduced to walking in single file, the absentee landlord leading the way, myself next, followed by Mr. Lo and the cultivator, after whom came twenty or thirty others bent on hearing what was being said.

My conversation with the landlord became increasingly exuberant, and rather *risque*. I had correctly assessed his *milieu* in the city. It was one to which I had on occasion been invited. I sensed the line of patter to be followed— patter designed to produce laughter and surprise that a European should know of certain questionable matters usually kept concealed from them. Mr. Mui was, in fact, after a few moments, laughing so gustily that, on one occasion, I had to put forth a rapid hand to prevent him from falling into a waterlogged field. He was exuberant beyond

47

measure, aware that, with such a magistrate, his case was as good as won.

Behind me was silence, save for the voice of Mr. Lo, who was also, I realized, familiar with the *milieu* Mr. Mui inhabited, and translated my remarks unhesitatingly. Mr. Lo was a man of the world; and a great asset that is in an interpreter. Such a one seldom falters.

It was the silence beyond to which I was really listening, though: a silence of pursed lips and hate, of something they might have known—that the magistrate would be on the landlord's side—though not surely to this extent, with all this talk about clubs and mistresses. . . .

We inspected the fields, where my predecessor's wisdom in suggesting a visit at once became apparent. As explained earlier, it was a region in which the sea was receding, with the result that the field area, which was very large, was extremely flat, and peculiarly difficult to irrigate. Water, descending from mountain streams, would only flow in certain directions discovered as a result of centuries of experiment. The rise of an inch in the level of the land, and water from quite a different stream had to be used, the whole forming a cross-pattern of various watercourses, intertwining to irrigate all.

The watercress beds, registered as belonging to Mr. Mui, were situated in what was, waterwise, the upper part of Mr. Mui's fields, which stretched for some distance beyond them in the direction of the sea. The watercress beds furthermore lay on the direct track of the irrigating water.

The cultivator wanted his fields to be continually wet for watercress. He did not, however, wish them to be flooded to the height essential for growing rice—the level for which the irrigation system had been evolved. He had thus made

48

a small diversion in the flow of the water, aimed at preventing it from flooding his watercress beds higher than was desirable.

One would have thought, to look at the diversion, that the water would reach the rest of Mr. Mui's fields. Instead, for some reason invisible to the eye, it did not. It drifted off into other people's fields, leaving the rest of Mr. Mui's land as dry as a board and useless.

We returned to the hotel in the reverse order: villagers, communists, cultivator and silence in front; interpreter, magistrate, landlord and cheerful laughter in the rear. In the restaurant, the management had lined square tables together in a double row, giving the effect of one long, broad table, down which chairs had been placed.

I took my place at the head of the table, with Mr. Lo on my left (the senior place); the landlord on my right; the cultivator, flanked by silently watching aides, farther down; as many of the rest as could find chairs, sitting where they would; the rest standing and packed densely all around us, their number now increased to about two hundred.

The mood of the people, which we had felt on first arrival, had intensified. As report of my friendliness with the landlord spread, it was verging on open hostility. It was Mr. Lo and I whose case was to be heard.

Mr. Lo, I had thought, had been translating readily enough my private conversation with the landlord. Not till we sat down, and I saw his face properly, did I perceive that, on the contrary, the course I had taken, and the result it had produced on the assembly, had made him uneasy.

I could not explain to him—lest it be overheard and understood by someone—but my disposition towards the landlord was the first step in a design. I did not pin much hope on it, but it was the only design I could think of, in view of the force assembled, coupled with the fact that we had come without even one police constable.

When power is overwhelmingly weighted to one side, an arbiter, if he is to maintain the independence of his position, has only one course to take, which is to throw as much weight as possible on the weaker side. It was my aim that the hearing should open with the Magistrate firmly of the landlord's party, with the cultivator and his aides feeling they were facing a high wall of opposition—a wall which the Magistrate knew was not nearly so high as it looked.

Mr. Lo was observably relieved when, opening the hearing, my tone with the landlord became more grave.

Mr. Mui, who was an important rice merchant in Hongkong, had inherited the fields from his late father, who had purchased them during the Japanese occupation, when land prices were low and (in that no one knew where the next meal was coming from) an acre or two of rice land was a useful asset. He had never farmed the land, always renting it to others.

Two years ago, Mr. Mui had gone on a protracted business visit to Singapore. He had not been away more than a few weeks before he received a letter from his wife in Hongkong to say that their ricefield tenant had not paid his rent. Unaccustomed to handling matters of this kind, the wife had not come over to the island to ascertain the exact situation. I doubt if she even knew where the fields were.

Mr. Mui, delayed much longer than he expected in Singapore, had been unable to take any measures to deal with the problem. He had returned to Hongkong a few weeks ago, he said, to find the defendant working part of his fields as watercress beds. When asked what he was doing, using the fields and paying no rent, the defendant replied that he had purchased the land he was using.

What had happened, apparently, was that the original tenant had absconded; but, before doing so, pretending he was the owner, he had sold part of the land to the defendant. Mr. Mui now wished to start farming the fields himself, but was unable to do so, not only because the defendant was illegally occupying part of his land, but because, in addition, the alteration to the watercourse had deprived the rest of the land of water. He requested that the court order the man to quit the watercress beds.

The cultivator, who, with his supporters massed around him, felt in a position to be offensive, said that the court could order what it liked, he would not leave his fields. If police were sent against him, he was prepared to lie down and die in his fields. He had bought them in a *bona fide* transaction, and they were his.

His utterances were dramatic, and their effect was telling. He had every man's sympathy. When he mentioned the police, too, and I observed the people's reaction, it brought out one of the underlying realities.

The truth is that these outer islands of the Pearl River were never really administered by anybody prior to 1898, the year of the lease. Without permission of authority, the ancestors of these villagers had installed themselves in the valley—in 1565, if I am not mistaken—and without permission their descendants had remained.

These people were the owners of this valley, in a sense which any government, Chinese or British, would have found it equally difficult to deal with. We with our laws were intruders—as Chinese officials with their laws would also have been—brought in on this occasion solely to protect another intruder, the landlord. Added to this, his watercress beds apart, the defendant was really and truly a landless cultivator, being descended from a family whose ancestors had entered the valley later than the rest, and who had thus traditionally worked as labourers on other people's land.

Completing his defence, the cultivator passed up to me with an arrogant flourish his deed of purchase.

It was a soiled piece of rice paper, about the size of a postcard. Written in semiliterate Chinese characters, it was a receipt for an unspecified sum of money. It bore two signatures, but was not dated, and gave no indication of the nature of the transaction.

Accustomed (as I was now gradually becoming) to an existence in which a man's word is his bond, and few agreements are ever committed to paper, the existence of any document at all surprised me. To those present, it was conclusive sign of the rightness of the cultivator's cause.

To my inexperienced mind, however, legal right seemed to lie entirely with the landlord. Accepting that the cultivator had been the victim of a confidence trick, he still had no legal right I had ever heard of to be on the land. With his sullen and verbally tempestuous determination not to quit, he faced me with the solution I most wished to avoid—having to use force to remove him.

I could see no alternative, however. In addition, with the throng of people all around us, in the full heat of June, the air charged with angry emotions, I found it extremely hard to think.

All I could see was a picture of what would happen if force were used. The watercress might have to be pulled up. From all five villages there would be resistance. There would certainly be violence, followed by charges of criminal assault. Mr. Mui might end up as the undisputed owner of the fields, but neither he nor any member of his family would ever with complete safety be able to set foot in the valley again. Finally, such an order, whether legally right or wrong, would throughout the valley darken the name of the district administration, and indirectly of the entire government.

Yet such, it seemed, was the way of law.

"Have you served notice to quit?" I asked Mr. Mui.

"No."

"Why not?"

"Because it would be tantamount to admitting that he is my tenant, or sub-tenant, which he is not."

What the precise legal validity of this was, I did not know; but it sounded sense. Mention of notice to quit, however, had reminded me of the custom of the district, which was that when a cultivator was so ordered, he was permitted an extension of notice until such time as his crops on the land had been harvested.

His crop was watercress, I thought.

I began to wake up. Watercress beds are always re-sown immediately a crop is sold. As our inspection of the beds had shown, the cultivator was using the three fields on a serial basis, so that at no time was there more than one field empty, and then only for a few hours.

"How long have you been growing watercress in your fields?" I asked the cultivator.

"Ever since I bought them."

It sounded convincing, and yet . . . watercress. It was the one crop which rendered most difficult the application of a notice to quit. The cultivator's choice of watercress seemed to me to be deliberate. I decided to try a little bluff.

"When was that?" I queried.

"Eighteen months ago."

53

"I see. Yet, eight months ago, before I went on leave, I came on a hike through this island, and passed those very fields.—Why was it that at that time there was nothing growing on them?"

"There was. I was growing watercress then."

"I suggest that is a lie. Those fields were empty."

There was dead silence throughout the room. I had been lucky. It was the truth.

"And why," I pursued, "was it that, when you bought the fields, the sale was not registered at my office?"

"I didn't know it had to be."

"Come now, you've lived here all your life; and you say you've never owned any land. This, your first purchase of a piece of land, must have been known to every man in the valley—to every man present here today. Any of them could have told you that a sale of land has to be registered in my office."

"No one told me," the man answered sullenly.

"I suggest no one told you, because everyone in the valley—everyone present here today—also knew that the man from whom you say you bought the fields was only a tenant, who had no right to sell them to you. Are you telling me that you were the only person in the valley who did not know that this man was a tenant?"

"I knew he was a tenant, but he told me the owner had given him the right to sell the fields."

"Had you given such permission, Mr. Mui?"

"Certainly not."

I returned to the cultivator.

"I suggest that from the moment of occupying those fields—in which you were originally growing rice, but are now growing watercress—you knew perfectly well you had no right to be there. I suggest further that, the rightful owner having returned, the proper and sensible thing for you to do is to crop the watercress you have standing, sow no more, and peaceably restore the fields to their owner."

"Not unless he pays me compensation for what I paid for them."

"How much was that?"

"Two thousand dollars."

This was a preposterously high figure. Mr. Mui laughed. Mr. Lo smiled as he interpreted. There was a general awareness among the crowd that their man had made a mistake.

The public reaction towards the three of us at the head of the table, which had been growing steadily more hostile as I questioned the cultivator, became knife-like before the signs of amusement his claim provoked. In another moment the situation would be out of hand. We had whittled the cultivator down somewhat, yet to no advantage in the final issue. Still plainly before us lay the use of force if we were to remove him.

"How much compensation would you be prepared to give this man, if he were to move off peaceably?" I asked Mr. Mui.

"Not one cent," he answered.

Here Mr. Mui made his mistake—not with the villagers, who expected such a reply, but with the Special Magistrate, who did not.

In the free and easy way of things, Mr. Mui could well have given the cultivator a present. Mr. Mui was a rich man; and it was his own fault, for not chasing up his tenant, that the situation had arisen. At the sight of him in his true landlord's colours, whether in the right or in the wrong, he ceased to enjoy much sympathy from me. And, thinking of that tenant of his, I woke up a little more.

"You said, Mr. Mui, that you went to Singapore two years ago."

"Yes."

"Shortly after which, your tenant ceased paying rent."

"Yes."

"And you said that you found out about this other man being on your fields on your return a few weeks ago."

"Yes."

"Do you mean to say your business visit to Singapore took two years?"

Mr. Mui's face was expressionless, eyes on the table.

"Not quite two years."

"Not quite, Mr. Mui? Exactly how many *weeks* were you in Singapore?"

"Oh, I was there several months."

"How many months, Mr. Mui?"

A calculation produced the fact that he had been away seven months.

"You thus returned to Hongkong about one and a half years ago, just about the time when this man was moving in on your fields. You knew about this, you say, shortly after your return; yet for a year and a half you did nothing about it. Why this sudden interest now?"

"I knew about it, but I had many other things to attend to. There was no time till now."

"You have also explained that the reason you want this man off your land is so that you may farm it yourself."

"That is correct."

"If you have so many other things to attend to that you can only visit it once a year or so, it will be an odd kind of farm, will it not?"

There was a ripple of scornful amusement around us.

"I don't intend farming it myself," the landlord answered. "I shall put someone on it to run it for me."

"I see."

But Mr. Mui's real motive had become clear. The area was developing as a fashionable locality for small country retreats. Around the flat rice area, there already existed a number of tasteful bungalows surrounded by small gardens of willow and bamboo, owned by men such as Mr. Mui. He had decided to join the fashion. In order to obtain land on which he would be permitted to build a house, he would have to bid at a government auction, at which the price was liable to be relatively high. The real reason Mr. Mui wanted his land free of encumbrance (the cultivator's watercress) was that he intended, in due course, to negotiate an exchange through my office, surrendering his agricultural land, and receiving in its stead a smaller piece of building-and-garden land, valued at the upset auction price. He would thus bypass the auction and, he hoped, come off with a bargain.

With a recent rise in the local price of building land, policy had taken a swing against exchanges of this kind, and though Mr. Mui did not know it, the exchange he had in mind was most unlikely to receive government approval.

I took a look at the cultivator. He had been undeniably dishonest—but surely no more dishonest than Mr. Mui, with his carefully rigged story, and his deceptions about wanting to become a farmer. And there was the cultivator, after all, born and bred in the valley, landless, and with nowhere else to go. There they all were, all two hundred of them. It was their valley. There should be a place for each of them in it.

"On this question of your farming your own land, Mr. Mui, it seems to me that these watercress beds are the

57

lesser of two problems. The more important problem is that, with the watercress beds where they are, by far the greater part of your land is without water."

"That is so," he replied. "This is the main reason I want this man off."

"If, on the other hand," I said, "we were to ask this man to shift his watercress beds from the top end of your fields to the bottom end, water would then flow properly over the whole area, and you would be able to farm the rest of it without any difficulty."

There was amongst the people a sudden, tense silence as this was interpreted. Nor was it any longer a hostile silence. It was excited, expectant. We were on to something. I went on quietly.

"This," I said, holding out the supposed deed of purchase in the direction of the cultivator, "is a worthless piece of paper. I suggest that what really took place between you and the former tenant involved no cash transaction at all. That man left here in a hurry, owing money, as we know." I turned to Mr. Mui. "If a proper financial arrangement can be arrived at between yourself and the defendant, would you be prepared to allow him to remain on your land, but at the bottom end, instead of the top?"

The silence continued. Every eye was fixed on the rice merchant. It was difficult not to feel a bit sorry for him. The silence spoke for itself. He was cornered by public opinion.

"He has no right to be on any part of my land," he said nervously.

"I agree with you entirely, Mr. Mui. What I am seeking is an act of generosity on your part, generosity which will be appreciated throughout the valley. I put it to you that your real position is that you know very well that it will be difficult to farm this land yourself. You are not a farmer, and have no experience of farming. You are the owner of this farmland, however; and because it belonged to your father, you do not, out of respect for your father, wish to part with it." (This was putting Mr. Mui's position in an unduly favourable light, but it was a form of reasoning everyone present would understand.) "You have already said that it would be your intention to put someone on the fields to farm them for you. I would even go so far as to suggest that this cultivator, who, as we have all seen, is a skilled farmer with no land of his own, would be just the man you are in search of. If," I continued, addressing the cultivator, "you first agree, here and now before all of us, to withdraw all that you have claimed about having purchased these fields and being their owner, would you be prepared, on a just and proper basis, to farm the land for the complainant?"

As these words came forth in Chinese, a low rumble of murmuring broke forth all around us. It was an extraordinary sound, urgent and emphatic, in the midst of which, from a dozen or more voices, I caught the injunction: "Accept! Accept!"

The cultivator, who, from the instant I had thrown his deed of purchase back at him had worn a dark and vengeful look, did not at once react to the impact of opinion directed at him from all sides. Behind him men were tapping him on the shoulder, advising him in urgent whispers to give in. This time it was he who was cornered by public opinion.

I must confess that never before or since have I had quite such an exciting moment in the course of a case. Leaning back in my chair, scarcely able to keep still as the deep, strident sound continued to envelop us, I tried to

59

take stock of the strange situation. By sheer accident, groping blindly forwards, we had arrived at a position of offering a solution which, by Western standards, was not only
illegal but immoral, yet which, though neither party entirely liked it, had unexpectedly touched upon an authen-
tically Chinese answer.

"Well—?" I asked the cultivator after a moment or two.

With a scowl, he agreed.

"Do you publicly withdraw all your claims to ownership
and compensation?"

"Accept! Accept!" whispered the voices.

"Yes," he replied.

"Mr. Mui—?" I inquired.

Mr. Mui gave a quick, sharp nod, such as I fancy his
own office staff must have seen many times in assent to a
business proposition. We had passed from the realm of
half-truths to that of facts.

"I congratulate you, Mr. Mui, on your generosity; and I
congratulate you too," I said to the cultivator, "on your
common sense, and also on your skill as a grower of watercress. If either of you require any assistance from my office
in coming to an agreement, or wish to register that agreement, our services will be at your disposal."

I rose. On all sides the villagers were drawing back,
beginning to disperse. Tension had gone.

There were no smiles as we left. Few compromises are
perfect enough to inspire happy faces. But the cynicism
and disdain which had greeted us had gone. The claims
had been balanced. There would be no violence. In fact, I
gauged, if we were lucky, we might never hear of the case
again.

Indeed, we never did—though what Mr. Mui said to
his friends when he went home to Hongkong I tremble to

think. Unless—and perhaps, on second thoughts, this is more likely—he said nothing.

For various reasons, the whole truth never comes into a Chinese court, rendering it singularly difficult to assess the rights and wrongs of any suit. But in a small community, such as the five villages in the watercress case, more or less everyone *knows* the truth, though they will not divulge it; and they can judge at once when a fair balance has been struck. From that day I learned the value of hearing cases before a body of *informed* public opinion. The public had solved that case, not I.

It had also shown me something which I do not think I could otherwise have discovered: that Chinese general ideas about justice are less concerned with absolute standards of right and wrong, in the context of specific laws and situations, than with a vague and diffuse principle of general benevolence, expressed perhaps in the words 'I have as much right to be alive as you'.

If, instead of pursuing hard and fast legal judgments—good for one party, bad for the other—one aimed for generally unsatisfactory compromises based on this imprecise principle of benevolence, there was a fair likelihood of unexpectedly harmonious results.

5

The Stranger

EVER SINCE THE NEW TERRITORIES settled down under British rule—originally, in 1899, there was a minor rebellion against it—the relationship between the administration and the people had been personal to a degree rarely to be found anywhere in the world, and certainly nowhere in China. The people of the New Territories have rightly been called China's spoiled children.

This does not mean that there was no poverty, or suffering, or social injustices. No society is perfect. But it did mean that any villager, however humble, if he had a justifiable reason for doing so, could come without fear to the magistrate, and receive personal attention. Ever since the lease was agreed to, it had been expected of every magistrate that he should, in the old Chinese phrase, be 'the father and mother of the people'.

Conversely, half a century of British administrators, most of them speaking fluent Chinese, had had their backs slapped, been joked with in ribald terms, feasted sumptuously, sometimes made terribly drunk, and been given all kinds of humble presents from the soil. As an example, in my first week a hunting friend of mine, a villager from the eastern part of the district, turned up in my office with half a wild deer he had just shot. It was really rather embarrassing; I could not quite see myself carrying it back to Hongkong by the public ferry. I hastily explained that I did not have a stove large enough to cook it on, whereupon it was taken to a nearby butcher, chopped into more manageable pieces, and we shared it (it was delicious).

The administration was not without its faults—is there any administration which is?—but the relationship between government and people was, I believe, unique on Chinese soil.

Refugees, newly settled in the New Territories, at first could not believe their ears. When told by their indigenous neighbours that, if they required a permit to start a duck farm, or build a small house, they should go personally to the appropriate district office, they were in general appalled. In China, if you wanted a quiet life, the very last place you went anywhere near was a government office. I have known refugees who remained six or eight months in a kind of paralysis before venturing near the administration, and who later laughed heartily at their own timidity.

I do not know how it was in the other districts, but in our office we found, curiously enough, that it was the educated who were the most fearful of coming to us, and who were the most surprised by their reception. For, dealing most of the time with simple country people, it was pleasant to relax for a few moments and talk to someone well educated. It was intriguing, too, to discover, as conversation proceeded, that one's visitor, who had come, perhaps, for a duck permit, was actually one of China's leading astronomers, or—as on another occasion—to find oneself talking to a renowned haematologist who, his degrees being unrecognized in Hongkong, had decided to breed quails. I made many delightful friends in this way, and so did members of the staff.

But, due to the tremendous increase in population, it was a régime which could not continue indefinitely. This fact was recognized in all three district offices, but in none more acutely than in the Southern District, where such a great amount of my own and the more senior officers' time had to be spent on ensuring the orderly development of our rapidly growing industrial zones. It became progressively more difficult to deal with the country people personally.

The trouble was, of course, that the villagers could not see why things should not go on as they had in the past. They continued to arrive in their hundreds—one morning, coming to the office half an hour before it officially opened, I counted eighty-three people standing outside, nearly all of them wanting to see me personally—and they often felt aggrieved when they were dealt with 'only' by a clerk.

To remedy this in some measure, I installed in my own room a young Chinese officer in whom I had great confidence, and who had worked with me before in the Secretariat. He became virtually my private secretary—or, as they say in Chinese, my 'confidential books'—and putting him in my own room meant that he was my proxy. Anything a visitor discussed with him was in my hearing, and people quickly realized that his word was my word, this being possible because he had an exact understanding of my methods, and of my ways of dealing with people.

As for the magisterial work, nearly everything had to be devolved on the two senior clerk-interpreters, assisted by two promising young juniors, whom I selected because of their tact and kindness, the two most important ingredients in a *personal* office, such as this was, and such as it had always been.

In due course we reached the stage where the only cases referred to me were ones in which the participants emphatically insisted on a personal hearing by the magistrate. (Those who so insisted proved almost without exception to be dishonest, thinking they would do better with a foreigner than with a member of their own race.) Cases deemed insoluble were also referred to me, the decision to throw them out being a responsibility which, for obvious reasons, I could not devolve.

Halfway up the long office passage, a gate was installed, beyond which no one was admitted, unless coming to see the land officers, the confidential books, or (by appointment) me. This was considered horribly severe. It brought to an end the old system whereby villagers drifted into the magistrate's office, and wasted hours of his time in tortuous explanations of their problems.

But I did not relent. Somehow the people of the district *had* to learn to trust their own Chinese civil servants, and begin at the bottom of the office,—a procedure they would certainly have to follow in the future, as the district became more and more connected with the expanding city.

Sometimes, however, I broke my own rules.

One afternoon, returning from lunch, I found the passage and all the offices literally packed with people, most of them villagers, men and women, intent on their own affairs, and difficult to move out of the way without actually pushing them.

One of the few who did move to allow me through was a man somehow different from the rest, quite tall, aged about thirty-two, bronzed and handsome in a gentle, quiet way, and looking as if he came from another province.

His eyes smiled at me as I passed. Chinese do not smile, as we do, when greeting unknown people; to do so is bad manners. Nothing in the man's facial expression had altered; but by looking in his eyes, it could be seen that they wore a smile. It was a look which I bore with me mentally as I struggled through the rest of the multitude, reached the detested gate, and entered the tranquillity of the more exalted offices.

"Po Wah," I said to the confidential books, "there's a man down the passage who's interesting, different from the rest. I wonder what he wants."

My *alter ego* gave me a steady look, nodded, and went out in the direction of the multitude. A minute or two later he re-appeared at the door.

"Is this the one?" he inquired.

Unerringly—knowing exactly what I meant by the word interesting—he had found the right man.

Seen alone, he was strong and well-built, a man of slow, easy movements; and he had a slight limp. I reckoned he was an ex-Nationalist soldier, and he told me he was from Hunan province.

He wanted to set up as a farmer, he said, and had come because he understood he would require a permit to build a hut for himself, and a toolshed.

My heart sank. We had all too many 'farmer' applications. The 'farms' usually turned out to be in semi-industrial areas, and the 'toolsheds' had a tendency to over-night metamorphosis into spinning factories employing twenty or thirty people in disgusting conditions of squalor, besides interfering with the industrial town plan.

"Where is your proposed farm?" I inquired guardedly.

He mentioned a rural area so remote that for an instant I thought I must have misheard him. It was a place at the extreme western end of the district, on a large island facing the Pearl River. Nearby was a hamlet called O Mun, consisting of six houses, all occupied by members of the same clan. He was proposing to rent some disused fields from them. The place was four hours' journey by ferry from Hongkong, and well over two hours more on foot from the

66

ferry pier. I had never before heard of a refugee knowing the terrain well enough to select such an isolated, but very fertile, spot.

"I believe the man's genuine," I muttered.

"I'm sure he is," said the confidential books.

"All right!" I exclaimed. "Let's help him."

Ancient land maps were produced, showing all property owned in the area. We found the six houses, and some fields; but where the man said his fields were, the map was blank.

"Are you quite sure there are fields there? Have you been there yourself?" I asked.

He had been there, and he was quite sure.

"Very well. We'll send a land demarcator to investigate."

Owing to the distance involved, this was a three-day job for one man. But he might be able to combine some other jobs *en route*; and so rare was it to find a genuine farmer that it seemed well worth it.

"He's a good man," said Po Wah, after the man had gone.

I thought so too.

A week later he returned, and the demarcator reported his findings. There were six disused fields where the man had said, and two ruined old stone houses. The bunds around the fields had fallen in at various places, but, with repair, all six could again be irrigated. The clan in the nearby hamlet claimed the fields and houses as theirs, but could produce no proof of ownership.

"Were the houses more than fifty years old, would you say?" I asked the demarcator, a chubby young countryman well liked in the district.

"Much more!" he exclaimed with awe, opening his eyes wide. "More like a hundred!"

67

The story of the property had clarified itself.

Once the people of the New Territories adjusted themselves to British rule—around the year 1900—they quickly discovered its advantages. Chinese imperial government traditionally discouraged migration of Chinese abroad, despite the fact that at least two provinces, Kwangtung and Fukien, had benefited from it considerably. Now, almost overnight, for New Territories inhabitants these old restrictions existed no more. They were free to migrate where they would, holding British passports, to which they became entitled under the lease. The result was that large numbers of the young and able quit their villages and sailed off to New York, San Francisco, British Guiana, Jamaica, Madagascar, Singapore, the Solomon Islands and a dozen other places. The depopulation of the New Territories was so acute by 1920 that there were numerous villages without an able-bodied man left in them. But the remittances which the men sent from abroad to their folk back home were a main source of the district's prosperity.

The original land ownership survey of the New Territories, started in 1900, took several years to reach remote spots such as O Mun, and by that time the vogue for migration overseas was well under way. The land and houses the Hunan refugee was interested in had once belonged to the clan at O Mun, but had evidently been deserted by the time the survey team came.

With the survey came the imposition of a nominal Crown rent, which many interpreted as the thin end of a wedge—which it was not—to subsequent higher taxation on land. The O Mun clan had thus not registered their ownership of the deserted property, hoping to save money. Due to this misplaced parsimony, they no longer owned the fields.

"How much rent were they asking you to pay?" I inquired.

"Twenty dollars a month," the refugee replied.

"Well, don't pay them anything. It's Crown land, and you can have the fields and the ruined buildings on permit from this office."

"I've already measured the land, sir," put in the young demarcator, who was another one who read the mind of the Special Magistrate.

"How much will the permit cost?" asked the refugee a trifle anxiously.

I glanced at the demarcator's sketch-plan.

"About six dollars a year, I should think."

Then, for the first time, he really smiled.

It was not a completely satisfactory arrangement, I realized. The clan, regardless of what the British land survey might say (it was only for ninety-nine years, after all), still considered they owned the land, having owned it under the Ch'ing dynasty. Under the lease of the New Territories, the only legal ownership the man could acquire quickly was the permit I had offered him; and I could not condone private payments of rent to the O Mun clan, who, so far as I was concerned, had nothing to do with the land in question.

In addition, I felt that the man himself would know how to deal with these *in situ* problems. He was quietly but impressively self-reliant.

As I was shortly to discover, I had been over-optimistic. A stranger in a Chinese rural area is rather more of a problem than one might think.

Some weeks later I had to pass through Saiwan, a 700-year-old township which was the nearest place of any size to O Mun. There was a police station at Saiwan, and it being the most remote police station in the New Territories, I always made it a point to call on the young European inspector in charge, who led a pretty lonely life.

On this occasion, I asked him if he had anything of interest to report. In these more distant islands the district administration was thin on the ground, and the police often passed us useful information on general matters.

"Nothing much that would interest you, sir," the young man answered, and then in afterthought, "Oh yes, by the way, there's a stranger who's moved on to some disused fields near O Mun. He says he has your permission."

"He has," I replied. Inexplicably, I found myself on the defensive.

"The villagers don't seem to like him much."

"No, I don't suppose they do," I said with feigned nonchalance.

The clan had been thwarted in their attempt to obtain rent from the newcomer, who was furthermore from another province; and in no country is it more difficult than in China for people of different provinces to live or work peacefully together. I had expected some teething troubles, but nothing much.

A week later, the *heung cheung*, or village head, of O Mun came to see me in Kowloon. He was an elderly man, gnarled, with close-cropped grey hair, and sad, hopeless eyes. They were a clan who had gone down in the world, their place having formerly been larger and more prosperous than it now was. It was a very long way for him to have come, and it boded trouble.

"There's a man squatting on some of our land," he said. "I told him to clear out, but he won't. He says he's been given permission by *you*."

He said it with scarcely concealed insolence.

"He *has* been given permission by me, and it's not your land he's on," I replied.

"It is our land."

"Show me your proof of ownership."

"Proof?" he said angrily. "What need is there for proof? Everyone knows we own the land."

"Everyone except us, old man. Those fields are not registered as belonging to anyone."

He knew it, and hesitated.

"Well, I want him off," he said gruffly. "He's a nuisance."

"What kind of nuisance?"

"You have no right to let him have our land!" he replied.

"Mr. Lo, tell this man politely to stop teaching me my business, will you?"

He did so, but it had no effect. It seldom does in anything concerning a villager and land.

"Tell him to move off," was all he said. "Tell him to go somewhere else."

"Where else is there in that area?"

"I don't know," he answered, dismissing it.

"Neither do I. Now look," I said, trying to reason with him, "I know that man isn't Cantonese. But that doesn't mean he's not entitled to occupy land. We have thousands of refugees from China on our hands, and somehow they have to earn a livelihood. Now, please be reasonable, and treat this man as a neighbour. He is doing you no harm."

The old man pursed his lips, and said in a low voice:

"If he stays, there'll be trouble."

"Is that a threat?" I demanded sharply.

He did not understand what this meant.

"Are you threatening to make trouble for that man?" I

71

asked. "Because if you are, let me warn you, we will make trouble for you in return."

There were various ways in which we could make trouble for people like this. The one I had in mind at that moment would be to check all their boundaries, which must certainly have expanded illegally over the past fifty years. There might be some illegal additions to buildings, too. This would involve the clan in a lot of comings and goings between O Mun and Kowloon, which would be annoying to them and expensive—enough, I calculated, to bring them to reason.

But the *heung cheung's* only reaction was to mutter something angrily to Mr. Lo, which the latter did not translate. It was evidently a refusal to speak to me any more, and must have been in pretty rough language.

"Old man," I said finally, "I am giving you a warning, so take heed. After our conversation today, if any harm comes to that stranger, I shall lay it at your door. Now go home and learn to be a good neighbour, and don't let me hear any more of this nonsense. At the end of three months, I will come and see you at the village; and if you still wish to complain to me, you may do so then."

I still could not help feeling that time would settle this matter. The Hunan man was not a trouble-maker, and since he had had the enterprise to settle where he had, surely he would find a way to being on good terms with the clan.

There was a personal side to it as well. Chinese provincialism, with its unreasoning intolerances, was a thing we saw a good deal of, specially in the industrial areas, and it invariably irritated me. I was determined that the stranger should remain on those fields.

The following week came an urgent communication, delivered by special messenger, from the police inspector at

Saiwan. There had been serious trouble at O Mun. Acting on information received from the chairman of the Saiwan rural committee (the most senior Chinese in that part of the district), police had been sent to O Mun two nights previously to protect the stranger from the villagers, who were threatening to destroy the hut he was living in, and break the newly-repaired bunds of his fields. Arrangements had been made for a police patrol to pass there nightly, but the inspector informed me he had not enough men to continue doing this indefinitely.

This I had to concede. The zone covered by the Saiwan police station was large, roadless, and extremely mountainous. Obviously the police could not afford to give continuous attention to a place as small and distant as O Mun.

But the tenor of the inspector's memorandum was plain: it was my fault all this was happening; why would I not see reason, and settle the man somewhere else?

The memorandum had to be filed, which meant it was seen by the staff. Once again, atmospheric changes over the next few days told me that the staff were of the same opinion as the police.

A Chinese staff is an extraordinary organism. It never speaks its reproaches; it simply sends out electric waves. 'This is all your fault," the waves said, 'you're inexperienced.' There was provincialism in it, too. My man was from Hunan, while the staff were all Cantonese. The Hunan man, as they saw it, was my favourite; and this was the kind of thing that happened when magistrates had favourites.

I was furious with all of them, but could say nothing.

Next, the Saiwan police inspector, evidently interpreting as indifference the coolly worded note I had sent in reply to his memorandum, telephoned me.

In those days, telephoning the islands was a terrible business. Only the police had telephones, an antedeluvian species of radio telephone, down which, even yelling at the top of one's voice, one was frequently inaudible.

"I've had the whole village of O Mun over here at the station!" yelled the young inspector. "This is the third time in a week! They're threatening to use violence! Sir, we can't go on like this! Can you come and see them?"

I glanced at my diary. Every single day was reserved for something.

"Not in under three weeks!" I yelled back.

"What was that?"

"AFTER THREE WEEKS!"

"But this is serious, sir!"

"I know!"

"What?"

"I said I KNOW!"

"Could you cancel his permit?" the inspector yelled.

One or two members of the staff, I realized, were listening at the door, the noise of my shouting having momentarily stopped all work. It was summer, and the telephone was wet with perspiration from the palm of my hand.

"No!" I yelled furiously. "I will NOT cancel his permit! He has *every* right to be *there*!"

"I beg your pardon?"

"I said, he has *every* right to be—"

And at this point the telephone broke down.

I felt helpless. How was I to protect my man? How was anyone to protect him? In that lonely spot he was completely at the villagers' mercy. And if anything happened to him, everyone would of course blame me for that as well.

In the next few days I received a visit from the chairman of the Saiwan rural committee, an elderly and respected man, a personal friend of mine, gently suggesting that I might grant the man land elsewhere. I remained obdurate. The police inspector meanwhile sent an aggrieved memorandum to his chief, the marine police superintendent in Kowloon, copied to me.

This brought to the office an enormous and magnificent European police officer—the superintendent himself—covered with silver braid and medal-ribbons.

"I know, I know why you've come!" I said, raising my hands defensively. "But there's nothing, *nothing* I can do!"

"It's not very fair on that young lad of mine out there, you know," he said; he was a pleasant, fatherly type.

"I realize," I conceded. "I'm sorry. But this is a question of *rights*. The man has the *right* to be on those fields. And furthermore, those people have *got* to learn to live together."

"So you're not prepared to shift him somewhere else?"

"No. Not on *any* account."

"What d'you want me to tell that young lad?"

"Tell him, just be patient. *Please* be patient. This *must* somehow settle itself."

As he went, I clutched my forehead. Next, I suppose, we would have the Secretariat on the line, knowing how things blow up from microscopic origins.

Actually, a week went by without any more being heard of the case.

Then, one morning towards noon, Mr. Lo came into my room.

"Could you hear a family case, sir?"

I was submerged in files.

"No, Mr. Lo, no!!" I begged. "Please deal with it yourself."

"They want to see you, sir."

"Oh, very well," I said irritably. "Bring them in."

I continued with the file I was working on. As I did so, four or five people came and sat before my desk. I glanced up at the two immediately in front of me, a young man and a young woman.

"Who are they?" I asked, signing my minute and dating it.

"They're husband and wife," said Mr. Lo.

I looked up at them again. As could be seen at a glance, they were an almost tragically ill-assorted couple. The husband was about twenty-three, short and of poor physique, his skin white and oily, with spots across his forehead, and he had a pronounced squint. He was wearing a cheap, ill-fitting European suit, and that he was unaccustomed to such dress was suggested by his tie, which was not tied properly.

The wife, on the other hand, was wearing the black silk of the country people. Aged about twenty, she had fine, healthy skin, bronzed by work in the fields. She had wide-spaced, truthful eyes, and held herself well; her hair was oiled and neatly tied, and she had—well, let's face it, the Magistrate was only human—inviting breasts. She was a truly comely country girl, clearly of better stock than her husband.

It had obviously been an arranged marriage; and it was a good example of how wicked parents can be to their own children. How any of the four parents concerned could have believed that such a boy and such a girl could be happy together defied imagination.

The husband, poor lad, looked as though he had never taken any exercise in his life, and did not know what fresh air was. The girl, as was not infrequently the case in the New Territories, clearly did all the work in the fields, which according to Western ways of thinking the husband should have been doing, and doubtless ran the house as well. Seen together as a married couple, each was the object of pity.

"They're village people, aren't they?" I said (though only the girl suggested that they were).

"Yes," said Mr. Lo.

"Well, what's the matter?"

The hearing of cases had by this time been systematized. Mr. Lo laid before me a huge leather-bound volume, open at the page on which he had recorded the subject of the case, the statements of the parties concerned, and such other information as was required.

It appeared to be a case of the utmost triviality, and my irritation with Mr. Lo at having brought it in increased. The husband was complaining that his wife did not spend sufficient time in the house.

I glanced up at the husband.

"You mean she's often out?" I asked.

His eyes avoided my gaze.

"Yes," he answered in a low voice; he was very nervous. He seemed a suppressed person, unaccustomed to speaking out for himself.

"By day or by night?" I asked him.

He was silent. I tried again.

"Does she come home at night?"

"Yes."

"Does she cook your meals?"

After same circumambulation, it appeared his mother cooked his meals.

"Then, what you're complaining about is that she's out too much by day. Is that it?"

"Yes."

"Young man, if you went out with your wife to work in the fields, you'd see more of her, wouldn't you?"

It was unkind to have said it; and being a completely un-Chinese concept, it made me look, in their eyes, an ignoramus. But somehow I couldn't withhold it. I don't like young men who don't work.

I resumed my reading of Mr. Lo's summary. This concluded with the husband's request that I order his wife to stay nearer the house, and not talk to other men.

Despite my irritation, I nearly laughed.

"Mr. Lo," I expostulated, "what on earth is all this about?"

Mr. Lo, who secretly rather enjoyed family cases, specially the more salacious parts of them, giggled and said nothing.

"Well, what other men has she been talking to?" I asked him.

"This one," he replied, indicating the man nearest to him.

I shifted my attention for the first time to the man seated on the girl's right, next to Mr. Lo.

It was the stranger.

I glanced along the line to the man seated next to the husband. It was the *heung cheung* of O Mun. The young man was evidently his son.

It became apparent what Mr. Lo—and the staff—were up to. This was *my* case. I had started all this trouble. Let it be I who sorted it out; it was nothing to do with them.

Being by nature somewhat short-tempered, family cases were not my *forte*. I was already in an irritable mood; in addition, it was nearing lunchtime, and I was hungry. I glared exasperatedly along the row of faces before me, until at the sight of the girl something inside me melted; and as

78

it did so, looking at them again, the story of the four of them unexpectedly came to life. Two or three simple questions confirmed its every detail.

I was familiar with O Mun from my Secretariat days, having sometimes stopped there for a drink while hiking in the countryside; they had a well of very clear water.

The young husband was a son of his father's old age; and the father had made a vow, shortly before the child was born, that should it be a son, he would never have to do any work in his life. This is a senseless kind of vow, since its effects on a boy are invariably deplorable; but some fathers never learn, and instances of such vows are still to be found in Chinese society.

The area was one where, by tradition, women work the fields, the men sitting about doing largely nothing, living on remittances from overseas. In many parts of South China, rice-growing is considered a woman's work. This is because there are long months each year when ricefields need little or no attention, and it is thus theoretically possible to combine rice cultivation with running a home and having babies. In such areas, men work in the fields solely at sowing and harvesting.

The cultivation of vegetables, on the other hand, is a man's job, since vegetables need daily, even hourly, attention, such as a married woman cannot give. O Mun being situated far from any market, vegetables were not an economic proposition. Thus men there did very little.

But the *heung cheung's* son was an extreme case. He had been brought up to do absolutely nothing, even for himself. He probably did not even know how to tie his shoe-laces. He was not prevented from leaving the house. Due to his father's vow, he dwelt in the house as a treasured possession, and, cared for by others all his life, felt no desire to leave it. The pathos of it was that this treasured possession had been born with a squint.

None of this had to be explained across my desk; the indications of it were already there, in the young man's European suit (the little lord), his pallor, his hands, his tie, and the way he shrank from my direct questions.

This was the man the lithe and healthy young girl had married—a boy rather than a man, who had perhaps not left O Mun more than twice in his life, had seen nothing and knew nothing, had never been to school, and who, even in the house, was a creature almost completely helpless.

The girl had come from her own village, a larger place with more life, to be virtually imprisoned in that faraway spot, in a dark, stone, one-roomed house, all but windowless, with its raised section in the rear, supported by huge beams. Though she was sometimes allowed to clean and slice vegetables, her mother-in-law did the cooking. Her only release was when she carried the plough, and drove the cow out to the fields.

They had been married a little over a year, and there were still no signs of a child. It looked very much to me as though the marriage had not been consummated; and if this guess was correct, I suspected a special reason behind it, possibly astrological, i.e. the *heung cheung* may have believed it would be unlucky if the couple slept together prior to a certain date. As the vow itself showed, he was in some ways a strange man; and he dominated his son completely.

Into this uneasy situation had come the stranger. Occupying a wooden hut, which he had built against the wall of one of the ruined houses, less than half a mile from the village, he daily cultivated the deserted fields, the last of which was almost contiguous with the last of O Mun's fields.

As appeared from the husband's evidence, the girl began to spend more time than usual tending that last field of theirs, the furthest from the village. A bramble hedge, not very high, supported by pieces of old coffin-board, marked the end of O Mun's fields. Beyond this passed the main footpath to Saiwan, and on the other side of this ran the first bund of the stranger's fields. Inevitably, the day came when he was working in the last of his fields, she in the last of hers, each silent, neither one looking at the other, each conscious of the other's every movement, and thus for hours under the grey spring sky . . .

It was one of those inescapable situations. The stranger was a bachelor and alone, having to do everything for himself, even cooking. Even in the office we had felt the attraction of his personality. The staff might be disapproving, but he had made an impact. How much more on that lonely girl, with her miserable marriage! In the silence of the open fields, she would have found his every movement disturbing.

If I am not mistaken, this situation of silence between them continued for several weeks. Then, one day, she spoke to him.

She spoke to *him*. This did not have to be explained. He knew who she was. He knew it would be dangerous to speak to her. He knew his security depended on obtaining the clan's goodwill. But occasionally he was obliged to be in the last of his fields; and whenever this happened, it seemed, he found her near him.

The father and son had now come to ask me to order her to remain nearer her house, and not to talk to him. The *heung cheung*, whenever he looked at me, did so in sullen anger. He did not ask me to expel the stranger, however; and I gained the impression that Mr. Lo had warned him not to, probably explaining that I was a difficult foreigner, and it would only make things worse.

As a European, the whole business made my hackles rise. The unreasonable possessiveness of Chinese marriage—the fact that this wretched young man could take it as a matter of course (which he clearly did) that he was in his rights to demand that I order his wife to obey him—made me furious.

"I cannot give such an order," I told them; "it would be ridiculous."

This aroused even the husband to speak.

"She must not talk to other men," he muttered, with the obstinacy of the weak.

It made me angrier still.

"There are no laws to prevent it," I answered. "You should have bought a slave, not married a wife, if that's your attitude. It's your business to keep your wife in order, not mine. And anyway, what wrong has she done?"

There was silence. I indicated the stranger:

"And what wrong has he done? Anything?"

There was silence for a moment, then the husband said sullenly:

"They must not speak to each other."

"You are a thoroughly unreasonable young man," I answered hotly. "If you were more kind to your wife, and treated her properly, you wouldn't mind whom she spoke to."

It was true, of course, that the young girl had courted all this trouble. But who in the world could blame her? And who was I to issue a preposterous order that two perfectly innocent people should be forbidden to speak to each other? If she had spoken to the stranger, so what? Did it automatically mean she wanted to sleep with him? I had seldom been more angry.

Being in a measure personally involved in this case (the stranger being my 'favourite'), I was unconsciously judging it by European standards. I believe I even spoke of women's rights. I certainly reminded them that no one was to be condemned till proved guilty. The result was that argument went on and on, and round and round, for a good fifty minutes, getting nowhere. The stranger endured it quietly, saying very little. The girl occasionally shot me a look of understanding. The *heung cheung* and his son held their own with brutish obstinacy.

One o'clock came, and from outside could be heard the swishing of feet down the passage, as people went out to lunch. The case showed no signs of ending, and I felt hungrier than ever.

During this time the confidential books, across the other side of the room, had been busily engaged, writing in a file. At five past one, still writing, and without looking up, he said in the subdued but carrying tones of a stage prompter:

"You'll have to give the wife a ticking-off, you know, sir."

I exploded.

"I *refuse* to give her a ticking-off! Why should I? She's done absolutely nothing wrong!"

There was a pause, after which, still not looking up from his file, the prompter gently warned:

"They won't go away till you do."

It seemed that he, too, was hungry. I was enmeshed.

It also brought me to my senses. Though I was a European, I was not employed to impose European concepts of justice and rights. I was a Chinese Magistrate, expected to deal with matters in a Chinese way, whether I agreed with this or not.

It meant delivering a homily. This was what they had come for, and in a sense it was a step in the right direction. At least they had not asked me to expel the stranger, though this was clearly what they wanted.

Homilies by this time had become standardized. We had delivered the more common ones so often that Mr. Lo knew them by heart. It was, for example, possible to turn away wearily from a case, and say:

"Mr. Lo, deliver the standard lecture on monogamy, will you?"

Which he would then do, beautifully.

There was a standard lecture on fidelity and wifely obedience. But looking at the girl, so patient and pretty, and myself feeling utterly out of sympathy with my own Chinese rôle, I had not the heart to direct Mr. Lo to deliver it. Instead, I gave a watered-down and much shortened version of it, which I hoped she would realize was not meant to be taken very seriously. As I spoke it out, I felt ashamed and wretched. I felt a perfect pig, in fact.

But as Po Wah had predicted, the atmosphere improved. The girl looked suitably rebuked, the father and son more content, and silently satisfied with themselves. At the end I turned to the stranger.

"If we try to find you some other fields in that area, would you be prepared to move?"

He looked me straight in the eye. Not a muscle of his face stirred, but his eyes looked terrible. He had trusted me, and I had let him down. He was a refugee, and I was his one friend.

"I've done a lot of work on the fields," he replied at last.

"I'm sure you have. But if I do everything to help you, would you be prepared to shift?"

I could see him calculate that he must give the right answer.

"Yes, sir."

I knew then for certain that he was an ex-soldier.

"Very well. I shall be coming to Saiwan two weeks from today. Meet me there at the temple at ten in the morning, and we'll see what we can do."

Father and son now looked revengefully satisfied, though it was clear the father still blamed me for everything. They departed in silence, and at last we went to lunch.

A fortnight later, on the appointed day, I went to Saiwan, but the Hunan refugee did not come to meet me.

The main hall of the old stone temple, situated in the centre of the town, was used for conducting public business. The venue gave an appropriately old-fashioned air to our proceedings. At the meeting of the rural committee, held at a long table laid from the temple door to the first of the altars (before which I sat), I noticed the O Mun *heung cheung* seated some way down on my right.

Saiwan was a friendly place, with a good committee; meetings there always went smoothly, many matters being settled in a short time. The day's business concluded, we were standing around chatting, while white cloths were spread over the table, and a rather alarming amount of brandy and other liquor was laid out, when I found myself in a group with Mr. Lo, my friend the chairman, and the O Mun *heung cheung*, who was talking rapidly. He had a curious country accent which was hard to understand; and it was not until the chairman, with a word of reproof, silenced him, that, looking into those sad, hopeless eyes of his, I realized they were livid with anger—anger directed at me.

"What's wrong?" I asked Mr. Lo.

"Much, I'm afraid, sir," he replied.

In the middle of the night just passed, the young girl had risen from her bed without awakening anyone. Going to the ancestral altar, she had laid upon it, directly in front of the tablets, a red paper with her name on it, informing the clan ancestors that she was leaving, never to return, formally severing her relations with their descendants. Taking up a small bundle of her possessions, she then noiselessly slid open the wooden bar across the front door, slipped out, and ran through the starlit fields to the hut of the stranger. By dawn, both had gone.

The *heung cheung*, talking angrily, directed towards me a good deal of gratuitous comment, which Mr. Lo did not interpret. He did not have to. As the embarrassed looks of the chairman and other committee members informed me, what the man was saying was, 'Now do you see what you have done to me and my family?' And it was said with that contempt peculiar to the New Territories: the contempt of a citizen for a government which, he considers, has appointed bad officers, coupled with the more deep-seated contempt of a Chinese for a foreigner.

"I'm very sorry," I said. What else could one say?

Actually, I was sorry, but not for him or his son. I was sorry that the stranger should have let me down. I was sorry that those fields might be for another fifty years uncultivated.

After four days the police informed me that the couple were hiding in another village on the same island. The place was well chosen; the clan which lived there were traditional enemies of the O Mun clan, and between them lay seven hours of steeply mountainous walking.

Moreover, the stranger had not let me down. After a

fortnight in hiding, he came calmly back, alone, to his hut and his fields. He had somehow made friends with a Cantonese who was a police constable somewhere in the city; and a day or two later, this man took a month's leave and came to O Mun (letting it be known somewhat clearly that he was in the police) to stay with his friend. Between them they dismantled one of the ruined houses, using the cut stone to rebuild the remaining ruin. My friendly demarcator, I suspect, also helped by obtaining the free services of a village contractor who was another of my 'favourites' (because his work was good) to help with the roofing; and between them they did a thorough job.

The clan, awed by the constable and (I fear) by a member of the Special Magistrate's staff, watched in silence. The Saiwan police inspector warned me that the stranger was in for trouble in due course.

Each month thereafter, the stranger would go away for a few days; and then, one autumn day, he brought the girl to his home. There was renewed uproar. Nearly the whole O Mun clan walked to Saiwan police station, and demanded that the inspector order the stranger to clear out. With the help of the chairman they were somehow pacified, but no one expected the peace to be kept for long.

Shortly after the Chinese New Year, I decided to visit two small villages situated on a promontory some distance beyond O Mun. In summer the easiest way to reach them was to go by launch and swim ashore. In spring the sea was too cold for this, so we decided to walk. It was about four hours from Saiwan. I was not looking forward to the visit very much, since it would mean passing through O Mun; and I feared this would be the occasion for a renewal of all the unpleasantness.

We reached Saiwan to find that there had been a routine change of police inspectors.

"Has there been any more trouble at O Mun?" I inquired of the new officer, another young European.

"O Mun?" he queried. "I'm sorry, sir; where's that?"

From the police station windows the hamlet could just be seen, far across the other side of the bay.

"Over there," I said. "D'you mean to say you haven't heard about the trouble there?"

"No, sir."

"How long have you been here?"

"Two months."

It was strange. I did not like the sound of it. It suggested to me that they had secretly taken the law into their own hands, and thrown the man out. It would be very easy to do.

I was travelling that day with my second clerk-interpreter, always known as Ah Kuen. Like Mr. Lo, Ah Kuen was very much a man of the world. He had travelled widely in South China, and done many different jobs in his time, before joining the Hongkong Government after the war. During the Japanese occupation of the South he had taken to farming, and was wise in the ways of the countryside. He was a man whose opinion I valued.

"What d'you make of it, Ah Kuen?"

"Can't understand it," he said. "Shall we see if the chairman has any information?"

The chairman, we discovered, had gone to Hongkong. We might have found another informant, but we had a time factor to reckon with. If we were to get back to Hongkong by midnight, as we had arranged, there was nothing else for it but to press on at once, and risk the consequences of reaching O Mun ignorant of the present situation.

I did not like it. I had a nasty sensation that we might be in for trouble, and so too, I think, had Ah Kuen. We did not speak much as we walked.

It was an unusually warm spring that year, and the weather was glorious, blue and still, so warm that, after an hour of walking, we were perspiring and shedding clothes. The sun was high above us as we neared the village.

We passed the stranger's fields and his rebuilt house. Red papers, pasted up at Chinese New Year, still fluttered on both sides of the door; but the door itself was shut. There seemed to be nobody about. I could not understand it. They had been there at New Year, evidently. What could have happened since?

As we neared the village itself, I regret to say I found myself in a state of funk, not out of any fear of bodily harm, but out of embarrassment. I had become far too personally involved in this case.

"Let's go straight on, Ah Kuen. We can stop here on the way back."

By evening, I calculated, it would be too late to stop; and we could thus avoid a confrontation.

Taking a side path, we skirted the edge of the O Mun fields, avoiding the village. We were mounting a low hill to a pass, which led to the promontory we were aiming for, when in the last of the O Mun fields we found a woman working. Since it was the *heung cheung* I particularly wished to avoid, there seemed to be no harm in stopping to pass the time of day with the woman.

Ah Kuen explained who we were.

"Oh, the Li Man Fu," the woman said with a smile at me. She seemed perfectly unconcerned by our visit.

We chatted for a while in a friendly manner, and then:

"Ask her if the stranger is still living in that house," I requested Ah Kuen.

"The stranger?" she said, with the same complete unconcern. "Oh yes, he's there."

At this moment an older man, bringing two cows back from grazing on the hill, joined us. He, too, when he learned who we were, was perfectly friendly.

"Ask if the girl is still living with the stranger, Ah Kuen."

He did so.

"Yes, she's there," the man answered.

It was extraordinary. There was absolutely no hostility towards either Ah Kuen or myself, and none in the way they spoke of the stranger. It was as if nothing had ever been wrong.

We were moving on, with a wave and a farewell, when the man, still referring to the couple, added:

"There's a child coming."

I stopped in my stride for an instant, and so did Ah Kuen. I felt the perspiration on my forehead suddenly increase. Two plovers were calling to each other in the hills; a breeze was rustling the grass. Our equilibrium restored, we continued on and upward.

"From the point of view of formalities, Ah Kuen," I asked at last, "how d'you think he did it?"

"Difficult to say," he replied. "Village customs vary so much. But I should think he gave a tea party to the whole village."

"Where would he have done that?"

"Probably in front of the *heung cheung's* house."

"But surely the husband wouldn't have attended, would he?"

"No. He'd probably remain in the house, or go out that day."

"And the tea party would signify the acceptance of a new neighbour."

"Yes."

We walked on some way in silence.

"D'you think that, in addition to the permit fee he pays us, he's also paying them rent for those fields?"

"Could be," Ah Kuen conceded. "But only very little."

"The Chinese Empire dies hard, doesn't it."

But a gust of wind caught us as we reached the pass, and my words were carried away.

"I beg your pardon, sir?"

"Oh, never mind."

Neither of us mentioned the real cause of O Mun's unexpected harmony. We did not have to. The tea party was simply the formality without which nothing in China is complete. The real cause, which had completely changed the situation, and resolved it, was the unborn child.

A life was at stake, and there was peace.

How many times, in how many different countries, have I heard men—particularly men—say that one of the great difficulties in having dealings with the Orient, or even understanding it, is that the Orient values life so cheap.

When people say this to me, I do not answer, because to do so would mean telling a long story. Having now told a long story, may I give the answer I always wish to give. After twenty-four years of living in the Orient, the Orient which does not value life as we do, is an Orient I have never seen.

91

'Take Down That Hill . . .'

'THE DUTY OF THE LOCAL OFFICIAL is to adjust matters between town and country, to harmonize clashing interests (i.e. mark out land, etc.): to control the building of houses, to train stock, superintend arboriculture. He should advance morality, encourage filial and fraternal piety, all in their appropriate times—and urge the people to obey the government and live quietly and at ease.'

This description of my duties was given by the philosopher-administrator Hsun Ch'ing in the third century B.C.; and the fact that, 2,200 years later, it was a description astonishing in its accuracy, testifies to the antique profundity of Chinese ideas on government, to the *finesse* and exactitude of those ideas, and to China's extraordinary changelessness. It also demonstrates the degree to which the New Territories were governed according to traditional methods, understood by, and acceptable to, the Chinese people residing there.

Each week, the greater part of my time was spent 'adjusting matters between town and country'. The town zone was expanding rapidly, to the community's general advantage; but the town officials, from the central government departments, had inevitably a one-sided approach to their work. To them it was Hongkong's industrial and residential development that mattered; villagers, to most of them, were mere yokels, and village interests were not worth serious consideration. My duty was to fight a rear-guard action against urban encroachment, and to protect agriculture and village life, wherever this was desirable and possible, in order that the country people should not suffer by too rapid social and economic changes. At the same time—as instanced by the detested gate halfway up my office passage—it was my duty to prepare the country people for the changes that inescapably lay before them.

Marking out land, 'to harmonize clashing interests', was a major feature of the office's work; not without reason were the junior land officers called demarcators. The control of all building in the district was my responsibility; and the district being an area of rapid development, this work as the district's Building Authority took up a great deal of time.

The training of stock was mercifully dealt with by the Department of Agriculture; but it was my duty to indicate the villages to which pedigree pigs, fowls, and other stock should be sent. It was also my duty to talk the villagers into an understanding of the importance of improving their livestock, and to ensure that all the necessary arrangements for the introduction of improved stock were carried out.

The superintending of arboriculture was as vital as it was in Hsun Ch'ing's day. Apart from its flat and fertile rice valleys, the district was extremely mountainous, with generally shallow soil. There were few rivers or high springs. The summer rains came in torrents, but in a few hours all this water was washed out to sea. Every one of the little streams feeding the rice and vegetable fields depended to some extent on the moisture retained in the watershed soil by the restraining influence of the roots of trees.

It may be asked why Hsun Ch'ing, carefully selecting stock improvement and arboriculture, made no reference to agriculture. Had he done so, he would have made himself look ridiculous in Chinese eyes. People do not have to be told they need to eat. But most people do need to be told about stock improvement, and about the importance of trees.

Every effort had to be made to encourage people to plant. trees on the hillsides; and here there was one great difficulty. The traditional cooking fuel of the countryside was grass. All over the hills, at any time of year, could be found women cutting grass for fuel, either for themselves, or to sell to others. Very young trees growing among high hill grass are hard to recognize; the women did not understand the importance of trees, and each year many thousands of young trees were lost to the women grasscutters. Planting thus demanded full-time vigilance. Arboriculture, while vital, was a demanding occupation; and without encouragement (and without the planter's knowledge that the administration would protect his rights) few would have troubled to undertake it.

As to the local official's duty 'to advance morality, and encourage filial and fraternal piety', I trust that enough has already been said. This moral aspect of the magistrate's work—that it was his duty to *advance* morality (Hsun Ch'ing's word is carefully chosen)—was the keynote to all else. The magistrate could not, as in a Western country, simply lean back and say, 'These people are immoral.' Almost like a priest, and very much like a preceptor, he had to teach them to mend their ways. He was not there to pass judgment on them. He was there to guide them into doing what was right and proper. The morality he advanced, moreover, was Chinese morality; and woe betide him should he forget it!

'Adjusting matters between town and country' was a particular feature of nearly everything that concerned the district's largest town, Tsuen Wan. Originally a group of eight eighteenth-century stone-built villages, situated in a particularly fertile rice-growing area, fronting a shallow bay excellent for prawn fishing, Tsuen Wan had in the space of a few years skyrocketed in size and importance, and was second only to Kowloon itself as an industrial centre. The demand for land there for industrial, residential and commercial purposes was prodigious. The land in which industrialists were naturally most interested were the surrounding rice and vegetable fields, where development and communications were easy, and where there was a good water supply.

These demands ignored the fact that the original eight villages, which still existed in a submerged state amidst all the industrial muddle, were still rural in character. Had the administration permitted them to do so, the villagers would have been willing to sell their agricultural land, since the prices being offered were good. But had they so sold, the outcome, while benefiting the refugee population (already an overwhelming majority), would certainly have been that the greater number of the original inhabitants would have ended up destitute, being people unsuited to industrial employment. Somehow every acre of cultivated land had to be kept in agricultural use as long as possible, to allow time for the original inhabitants to adapt themselves to the new environment which had quite suddenly installed itself around them.

A particularly striking example of what this entailed occurred when I had only been in the office about a fortnight.

The conflicting demands of industrialists, property developers, government departments (waterworks, fire brigade, education, medical and health services, marketing, roads and bridges) and public utilities (electricity, telephones, gas, buses and ferries) were so confusing that it was impossible to understand them simply by studying maps and reading files. I had thus gone out by car with the land officers in the hope of gaining a general impression of the area (which I knew fairly well, but had never had to consider from this particular angle) and perhaps finding some solutions to our problems.

We stopped the car on the main road, about half a mile from the town, and from a nearby incline surveyed the scene. Before us, sideways to the shallow bay and the sea encrusted with gaunt, green islands, lay the tangled town. At the edge of it, on the landward side, rose a solitary hill, on the top of which the Department of Education was proposing to build a large and urgently needed government school. Beyond and around the town and the hill, and reaching to where we stood, lay the cultivated fields, the rice already standing high and freshly green. Closer to the town lay innumerable vegetable plots, laid out with loving precision. In many of them, the minute figures of men could be seen, toiling with their wooden buckets of urine, supplementing the winter fertilization of the soil with human faeces, the most valuable of all fertilizers—the *great* fertilizer, as the Chinese call it.

Inland still, the level of the fields steadily rose, mounting amid the trees of concealed villages and Buddhist monasteries, before sweeping upward in grass-green majesty to the summit of Taimoshan (Big Hat Mountain, 3,161 ft.), the highest point in the New Territories.

As in so many parts of the district, it was a noble and majestic view. But, as the distantly-heard whirring of machines told, it was a view destined greatly to change.

Our immediate problem that day was a desperate need

for more workers' apartments and shops. We needed the equivalent of three parallel streets of multi-storeyed buildings stretching the full width of the town. Actually, the entire centre of the town (the eight original villages, and the mass of squatter construction which had gone up amongst them) was by this time such a slum, besides being land wastefully used, that there was no alternative to pulling the whole lot down. But this could not be done until there was alternative accommodation for the people living there— the three parallel streets. Unless we took some more fields, it seemed plainly impossible to create those streets.

The land officers around me were discussing various alternatives; but it all seemed so hopelessly difficult that my mind had temporarily wandered away from the subject. I was thinking how pleasant the hill would look with the school on top of it, and making a mental note to request that the architects be sure to submit an attractive design.

This led me to start imagining the school itself. As a boy I disliked having to go to school, and left at the earliest opportunity—at sixteen, when my parents finally acceded to my pleas. Mentally I now saw myself as a small Chinese boy going to that school yet to be, lugging my books up the hill under the hot summer sun, reaching the classroom wet through with perspiration, my shirt crumpled and untidy, and in that state having to struggle to pay attention to some boring lesson, of no relevance to the kind of life one might one day expect to lead. I knew I would hate that school, and so would many a Chinese boy. It is only the rare teacher who can command interest under such conditions.

The land officers were still talking, when at this moment I interrupted them. "I think I see now what we ought to do."

My senior land officer—the burly, jovial European— looked down at me from what seemed a great height. He was a rather formidable man, and I felt for a moment as though I had said something indiscreet. I pulled myself together, and tried to sound authoritative.

"Yes," I said, and pointed in the direction of my imaginings. "Take down that hill, and move it by truck down that side-lane which leads to the sea. Dump the hill in the sea right in front of the town. That will give us the three streets we need, I think; and on the flattened site of the hill we'll build the school."

Beneath the blue sky of heaven it sounded unheard-of presumption. I could scarcely recognize my own voice, and was frightened lest the answer to my order be a guffaw.

Instead, the senior land officer assessed the size of the hill.

"Yes," he said, after a moment. "That would just about do it."

It had not occurred to me till then that, of course, land officers in the Hongkong administration were far more accustomed to hills being moved about than I was. The level area of Kowloon, after all, is in reality seventy flattened hills.

So thus it was. Less than two years later, the hill had completely disappeared. Three new streets, with intersections, had been paved on the Tsuen Wan waterfront, where the whole place was a soaring mass of scaffolding. And on the edge of the town, there were the boys, more than five hundred of them, coming to school each day without a bead of perspiration on their brows.

'Adjusting matters between town and country' is in general a headache, and can be a nightmare; but it has its enjoyable moments. And few, surely, would deny that it is pleasant to have the power *literally* to move—well, no—hills.

7

The Refugee Lovers

I THOUGHT IT ADVISABLE to give the foregoing description of Tsuen Wan, the district's largest town, and of the administration's work there, since some of the magisterial cases I shall describe, including this next one, were from Tsuen Wan, and the conditions of living which the cases reveal might at first give the impression that the place was a neglected slum and a social disgrace.

Actually, the intensive development of industry in the area was less than two years old when I took over the administration, and had resulted in a sudden inundation of population, mostly people shifting from squatter areas in Kowloon in search of work. The movement was irresistible, and was all the time continuing, producing social conditions closely resembling those of Kowloon and Hongkong during the refugee influx of 1949. Tsuen Wan's conversion into the modern industrial town it has since become had already started under my predecessor, and, as the anecdote of the hill perhaps suggests, steps towards improvement were proceeding at a fair rate. Meanwhile there were numerous slum areas, and it would take several years to clear them up.

Among the many cases which came to us from such areas, one I particularly remember. It was a divorce case. Mr. Lo had assembled the facts beforehand, and so certain was he of the outcome that he had brought in, in addition to the participants, the heavy leather-bound volume in which divorces were recorded.

They were a refugee couple, Cantonese residents of Shanghai, the man in his early thirties, the woman in her late twenties. They had met in a densely packed train bringing refugees southward. Squashed in like sardines, they had had places side by side, and at night there were no lights. On arrival in Hongkong, they had stuck together and struggled together.

They lived in the densely populated centre of Tsuen Wan, where they had a hut made of the usual miscellaneous assortment of scrap, with a tin roof secured by pieces of wire. The hut was constructed against the side wall of an ancestral temple, in a stone-paved street too narrow even for two bicycles to pass, part of one of the eight original villages of which Tsuen Wan was formed.

Sanitary conditions in these old parts of the town were indescribable. In their hut this couple had lived for four years, sharing it with pigs, out of which the husband made part of his income; and there the wife had borne him two fine, healthy children, who were brought along to the office, the elder a girl, the other an enchanting little boy about a year younger.

The husband was a strong, quiet-spoken man, with wide, honest features and golden skin. He did not look pure Cantonese; I fancy his mother may have been from Chekiang province. He was that eminently reliable type of Chinese, at sight of whom, in poverty or distress, you instinctively wish you could find a job for in your garden— if you have a garden, which in Hongkong is a rarity. He was obviously good with animals, flowers and children.

The wife, high-cheekboned, hard-faced and pale, was pure Cantonese. She moved elegantly. There was something brazen about her, and something sly. Mr. Lo's face did not alter when he looked at her, but I had begun to learn to read indications in that unaltering face of his. What it expressed at sight of this woman was irremovable distaste.

Despite the frightful conditions in which they lived, both the husband and the wife, wearing clothes that were all but threadbare with washing, were spotlessly clean, while the bonny, well-fed children spoke for themselves and the whole family.

Observing Mr. Lo's reaction to the wife, and wondering what had transpired between them all in the outer office, my instinct was to give the wife the greatest measure of benefit of the doubt which had assailed me, too, the instant she entered the room. She was not to be helped, however.

"You look after your children very well," I said.

She sniffed and said nothing; and looking by chance in the husband's eyes, I realized it was he who looked after the children. After no more than a few minutes, I had come to the conclusion that the woman was very lucky to have been able to string along with such a man as she had.

The husband was asking for divorce, and by the quiet, patient way he went about it, answering each question to the best of his ability without exaggeration, it was evident that trouble had existed between them for a long time. The husband had reached the limit of his sorely tried patience.

Even from their first months together, the wife had been going out with other men, while the husband was away at work (among other things he was a casual hawker); but until recently she had always returned to the hut to cook the evening meal. Six months ago she had refused to cook any more. The husband had been cooking for them all. Ten days ago she had left him. He was desperate, because with the children to look after, he could not leave the hut for long, and was not earning enough money to keep himself and them alive for more than a few days. It was essential that he be able to resume his hawking.

Questioned, the wife made no attempt to conceal her vagaries.

"I go with whom I choose," she said contemptuously.

It was clear she had come to despise her husband absolutely. He had perhaps been too gentle with her, too long-suffering.

The path which the woman was taking towards her own self-destruction was so plain that, as so often in divorce cases, I felt the first step was to do everything possible to keep them bound together. It was the woman's only hope.

"If she came back to you now, would you receive her?" I asked.

"Yes," he said quietly. "But she must behave herself."

"I will not come back," the woman said.

"What will you do about the children?" I asked the husband.

"I've found a woman," he replied, "the wife of a friend of mine, who has agreed to look after them during the day, if I pay her."

"You can afford that?"

"I shall have to."

It was not mentioned, but at the back of my mind, and I think at the back of the husband's too, lay the thought that the children might not even be his own.

It bore all the marks of being irreparable. Even if the wife were ordered to return, which she could have been, it would provide scant solution. Whether a man lives in a hut with pigs or in a palace, a wife's desertion is the same. He had been bitterly wounded.

"You realize," I said to the wife, "that if you do not

return to your husband, the law is that you must take and maintain your little girl, while your husband will keep the boy."

In a case of desertion, this was not strictly Chinese law; but it was the law used in that convenient form—the warning rattle.

"Yes," she replied, unperturbed.

I looked at the two angelic children. Seated one on either side of their mother, they were staring at me wide-eyed, wondering what it was all about. The adult composure of the little boy was remarkable; he was very young indeed. But as my eyes rested on him he took fear, and without shifting his eyes from me, moved his podgy hands till they found the comforting reassurance of the touch of his mother's dress.

"D'you mean to say," I said to her gently, "that you're prepared to go away permanently, and leave that child?"

Her body stiffened. Her dark eyes flared. She looked down with contempt at the little boy, before returning her gaze to me.

"I don't want him!" she spat out.

Mr. Lo frowned. An irrelevant, but so very human, element had intruded between the two of us. He hated a European to witness such a thing in a woman of his own race. Our eyes met for a second, then mine returned to the woman.

It was the face of a tigress, hungry with passion and desire. Among us there had entered, invisible, another party to the case, a man, the urge to unite herself with whom had drained this woman of all humanity, leaving her, in the physical sense, like an empty shell, incapable of containing anything other than the consuming flames of passion. This time it was no mere casual relationship she had formed. Her eyes seemed actually to project an image of the man across to me. Before we had done, I felt I knew all about him—more than I wanted to know. As a liaison, it too was doomed to failure.

Before desire so intense, laws melt away and magistrates are powerless. Had I been able to counsel six months' delay, I believe it might have been possible to have avoided separating those children from the mother they loved, and whose faults they did not understand. Much depends on the time at which people seeking divorce come before you. Sitting there, quietly listening to them, you can often see, more clearly than they ever will, what is likely to happen to each of them. If you can fabricate an excuse for delaying, until some of those things have happened, you can sometimes save a marriage. The problem begins to disentangle itself. People are wiser than laws.

In this case no delay was possible. The woman who was to look after the children was frightened of the wife, by whom she had once been violently attacked. A condition of her helping with the children was that the wife must no longer have the right to enter the hut. The husband had no pig ready for sale. In a few days he and the children would not have enough to eat.

One of the most widely held misbeliefs about the Chinese is that they are as their outward appearance suggests—contained, controlled people, whose emotions and passions are less strong than in other members of the human race. I had long come to believe the opposite to be true: that the Chinese, beneath their reticence and self-control, are among the most passionate people on earth. Not till that day, looking into the terrible eyes of that woman, did I realize that my conclusion had still fallen short of the truth.

"You are prepared to keep the daughter as well?" I asked the husband.

"Yes, I would like to."

"It would be better."

And so, as Mr. Lo had rightly foreseen it would be, the heavy leather-bound volume was laid on my desk and opened, and those two human beings were sent on their separate, hard and difficult ways.

8

Wall of Revenge

THE MOST DENSELY POPULATED part of the district, containing nearly half its total population, was the Kowloon urban area immediately north of Boundary Street, where the New Territories begin. North of Boundary Street was indistinguishable from south of it, but technically, north of it was called New Kowloon—though had one asked for New Kowloon in the streets, no one would have had the faintest idea what one was talking about.

All land transactions north of Boundary Street were registered in our office, but apart from this, we had very little to do with the area. In property cases, my jurisdiction as a magistrate was limited to properties worth $20,000 or less (the value of a sizeable stone house in country style, together with the land attached to it), and though such properties still existed here and there in the zone, the life of New Kowloon had become so completely absorbed in that of urban Hongkong that, as a matter of course, people resorted to solicitors and barristers, and had their cases heard according to Hongkong British law in the urban Courts of Justice. Similarly, family cases and disputes went to the urban Secretariat for Chinese Affairs, rather than to my more rural office. It was an inevitable consequence of the spread of the city outwards into the district.

One day, when I had been a magistrate for about eighteen months, Mr. Lo came into my room with a grin, which I took to be a grin of pleasure. Actually, he was pleased; but, as will appear, this was not all there was to it.

"We've got a case from New Kowloon, sir," he exclaimed, "the first we've had for years."

This was indeed very satisfactory, and admitted, so far as I could see, of only one interpretation. The fame of the Special Magistrate had spread. People had begun to realize that he was not just a petty official employed to look after rustics; he was the titular head of New Kowloon, to whom people could properly come with their problems.

"Do come in!" I said with an expansive gesture of welcome. I don't think I ever began a case in such a good mood.

Only one man came in. He was of medium height, middle-aged, and unusually lissome; his skin was golden brown, he had lively eyes and a ready smile. His close-cropped hair, turning grey, and his easy body movement, suggested a retired athlete. To my surprise, Po Wah recognized him instantly, and between them, he and Mr. Lo explained that our visitor was a retired movie actor, well known and once very popular among the Cantonese for his portrayal of villain rôles.

Music and the theatre are the world in which I was born, a world in which, regardless of race or tongue, all in a certain sense speak the same language. I already numbered among my Chinese acquaintances one or two leading actors and actresses, and inevitably at this moment, ignoring the object of my visitor's call, the two of us plunged into a discussion on the theatre. Our friend spoke a racy pidgin English and was an altogether delightful character, the perfect 'charming villain' type. Having fallen on hard times, he had given up the movies, and now lived in New Kowloon where, as he explained with a wry grin, he made a living fortune-telling, selling joss sticks, and carving name-seals. He was a man after my own heart.

Finally, we got down to business.

The actor had come, he explained, on behalf of himself and fifteen other neighbours, to complain about a brick wall which someone had built through a row of sixteen wooden shops, one of which was the actor's.

"What d'you mean, *through* the shops?" I asked.

"Just that, sir," the actor replied. "Right through them."

"Through them? I don't understand. Just where is the wall?"

"It runs through the middle of each shop, sir."

"You mean, it's a wall dividing each shop into two?"

"Yes, sir."

"Then you mean there are sixteen walls, one down the middle of each shop?"

"Oh no. Not divided *that* way. Divided the other way. It's one wall running through the middle of all sixteen shops."

"But there must be doors or gaps in it?"

"Oh no, there are no gaps."

I scratched my head.

"How high is the wall?"

"More than eight feet high."

It was incredible.

"Are you trying to tell me that you can't get from the front of your shop to the back?"

The actor nodded.

"That's it, sir."

The shops were situated in a congested squatter area. Only a few years ago it had been out in the fields. Since the refugee invasion from China, entire streets (untarred, because unrecognized by the government) and rows of little wooden shops and houses had developed there.

The sixteen shopkeepers in question had been living there peacefully for several years, when one afternoon a contractor and his men arrived with a truckful of bricks and cement, and began to build an eight-foot wall right through the middle of each shop. Equally amazing, being Chinese, the inhabitants let them carry on.

For several months now, after making a sale in the front part of the shop, the shopowner, in order to reach the cash desk at the rear, had to walk right down to the end of the row of shops, then all the way back on the rear side, to re-enter his premises by his back door. Similar journeys had to be made whenever anyone wished to eat, wash, or change their clothes, while, for security at night, families divided, some members sleeping for'ard of the wall, others aft.

One shop, it was explained to me, had a roof slightly higher than the others. In this shop a small boy, with the aid of two ladders, was just able to squeeze between the top of the wall and the rafters, and make direct contact between the two ends of his house.

"But who built the wall?" I asked in amazement.

"The landlord," the actor replied.

"The landlord? What for?"

"To make us pay more rent."

It seemed a strange way of going about it.

"All the shops are illegal structures, I suppose?"

"Yes, sir; I'm afraid we're all squatters."

"Understood," I said. "But this is ridiculous. People can't do things like this."

"I know," replied the actor with a mournful grimace. "But he *has*!"

It was a nice introduction to the problems of New Kowloon.

"Please try to help us all," the actor begged me as he rose to leave. "You're our last hope."

"Your *last* hope?" I queried. "Why do you say that?"

The real meaning of Mr. Lo's grin as he entered then became apparent. The shopowners had engaged a succession of solicitors in their efforts to have the wall taken down. A senior barrister-at-law had taken up the case. It had been heard in chambers by one of the Judges. There seemed to be no end to the number of people to whom the case had been taken. All to no effect. The wall still stood.

"You'll be telling me next the Chief Justice knows about it," I said with irony.

It was irony misplaced. The actor merely nodded.

"Oh yes, he knows about it," he replied.

It was going to be a tough case to handle, that was certain. But I saw what Mr. Lo meant. Where solicitors, barristers, lesser judges and greater judges had all failed, these sensible shopkeepers had turned to the Special Magistrate. It was a really very satisfactory morning.

From the land registers we obtained the landlord's name and address, and I sent for him.

He was an old-fashioned type, wearing a grey Chinese jacket buttoned to the neck, and getting on for fifty. He had a high, domed forehead, and was going bald; his eyes were cold and expressionless, his lips obstinate and cruel—altogether, rather what one would have expected. Once, long ago, I reckoned, he had been a mother's boy; or, perhaps nearer the mark, he had been brought up by amahs,* and thus shielded from many normal human con-

* Women servants, generally unmarried and sometimes vowed to celibacy.

tacts. Though he was extremely tenacious, there was little about him that was manly.

Many years ago, before the war, he had rented what was then a field from the real landowner, who was an Indian doctor resident in Hongkong. Part of the original boundary of the field ran along the exact line on which he had built the wall. He coolly denied that his aim was to obtain more rent from the shopkeepers. They had encroached on his land, he said, and he wanted them off.

"But the whole of your land is covered with squatters," I said. "Are you doing anything to get rid of the others?"

He merely repeated that he wished the sixteen shop-keepers to move back off his land.

"So you propose to do nothing about the others," I pursued. "You just want to make trouble for these people. Is that it?"

He was silent, but his cruel lips seemed to wear a smile.

"I suppose the others are more satisfactory with the rent they pay you," I said caustically.

Beneath the domed head, the cold eyes stared a fraction of an inch below mine—he never looked anyone straight in the eye.

"I take no rent," he said.

This was, of course, a lie. Among all the hundreds of thousands of little houses and huts erected by refugees on private land, it would have been difficult to find one which had not gone up without someone's permission, or without rent being paid. Chinese squatters are not that silly, neither are Chinese landowners.

For some unfathomable reason, the man wished to make trouble for the sixteen shopkeepers, and for none but them. No argument I could think of would make him budge. He seemed to me to be a monster of unreason.

"We shall get nowhere with this man, Mr. Lo," I said in the end. "Call up the doctor who really owns the land, and let's see if he can help."

Dr. Madan—the combination of his name and his softly-rounded features indicated that he was from Hyderabad, Deccan—was elderly and benevolent; but having lived for many years in a society 99 per cent Chinese and 1 per cent the rest, he had learned the importance of standing up for his rights.

"Those squatters are not my responsibility!" he said in a loud and high-pitched voice, almost as soon as he was in the room.

"Nobody said they were," I replied, recoiling slightly, and wondering whether I should repeat Queen Victoria's admonition to Mr. Gladstone to remember that 'we are not a public meeting'.

"I bought that field for my cows!" he explained vigorously. "And my understanding with that man was that he would use it for cows!"

"He holds the land from you on a 21-year lease, due to expire in eighteen months," I observed.

"That is so," Dr. Madan agreed, his high voice reverberating round the room; "and I want the field returned to me in the state it was in when I leased it to him! You see, Mr. Coates, I am very interested in cows—cows of a kind you have never seen. They are called Brahmin cows, and they are from India."

"Dr. Madan," I murmured, "I am familiar with India."

"These cows," he continued, taking no notice, "give milk of very superior quality. The importance of milk is not understood in Hongkong, particularly by the Chinese. Milk is an important ingredient of nourishment."

The actor, seated beside Dr. Madan, gave me a cautious wink.

The whole thing was more like a dream than reality.

"Did the field originally have a wall round it?" I inquired.

"It was partly walled and partly fenced. It was for my *cows!*" the doctor reiterated with a flourish of hands.

The fact of the matter was, of course, that the field would never be a field again. Within a few years, as the government's enormous refugee housing scheme was extended, the area would almost certainly be required for blocks of apartments. The government would then have to re-enter the land, and this would entail valuable compensation to landowners. Everyone was aware of this, though no one was so indelicate as to mention it.

The whole situation, however, was such a tangle of illegalities that it was hardly surprising it had baffled the legal profession. The doctor, in not having taken legal action against his tenant, had condoned the illegal structures. The tenant was making as much money as he could out of them, while the going was good, and no one could stop him. The squatters had no legal rights of any kind.

The doctor agreed with me that the wall was an iniquity, but insisted that he could do nothing about it, since his tenant was, in fact, merely replacing a wall which had once existed, but had been dismantled.

The only possible course, it seemed to me, was to appeal on moral grounds to the dome-headed principal tenant.

First, I inspected the site. Though it was a shanty town, it was considerably better than some of the others I had seen in other parts of New Kowloon. The sixteen shops were fronted by quite a well-defined 'street', and the shops themselves, and other constructions nearby, most of them wooden with tin roofs, were reasonably well built. Public water-taps had been installed, and there was some 'street' lighting.

It was dusk, and many people were having their evening meal. The actor met me, and together we visited each of the sixteen shops. It was all exactly as he had said. There, halfway up each shop, was this astonishing wall. Wives shouted out from beyond it that food was ready, and people in front set out on long journeys to get it. One wife, more accommodating, brought the food all the way round herself, arriving in front with it in a tiered pressure-cooker, as if she were going for a picnic—which, in a sense, she was. I found myself shaking my head in amazement.

All the shopowners were very friendly, and as sincerely anxious to have the matter settled as the actor. A group of them came with me as we went from shop to shop, and by the time we sat down in the actor's shop, amid stacks of joss sticks and boxes of hell money (to be burned for the use of the dead in the nether regions), quite a crowd had collected.

Several people had joined us from other parts of what should have been the field of Brahmin cows. These confirmed that they were paying rent for the land they occupied, but could not say exactly to whom (this was not unusual; payments were in cash, and the *rentier* seldom came himself); they also confirmed that no one had tried to increase their rent, or threaten them with eviction. It pointed to what I had earlier thought: that the landlord was out to make trouble solely for the sixteen, ignoring the rest.

If, in building the wall, the landlord had had a motive of revenge, or any other personal motive, against one or several of the shopowners, I felt certain they would by this time have split. For example, those who had perhaps given offence to the landlord would have been persuaded by the others to resolve their differences; and had they declined to do so, others in the group would no longer have co-operated with them.

As my visit showed, nothing of this kind had happened. The sixteen had fought this case united, through months of disappointment; and it was as clear as daylight that they were still united.

This, in my view, ruled out any personal motive on the part of the landlord, darkening still further the impression of himself which he had given me. The man's sole purpose, evidently, was to cause hardship and misery to someone— anyone—and he had chosen these sixteen families. It was a case of real iniquity—wickedness without reason behind it.

"Why don't you just tear the damned thing down?" I exclaimed at one point.

Several of them looked worried, and the actor shook his head.

"We couldn't do that, sir. He'll only do something worse for us. We must go through the proper authorities."

"But the proper authorities have been floored by it," I protested.

The actor grinned, and looking me straight in the eye, replied in the way of the country people:

"Not yet, Magistrate."

There were smiles and hope all round in the shop, and others echoed the actor's words. They had hitherto over-looked the fact that they were living in the New Territories. Having at last come to a New Territories official, they felt confident the matter would now be settled. The welcome they had given me, their goodwill and hope, and their confidence in me as a person (for everything to do with Chinese government is personal to a degree unknown in the West) were delightful, but embarrassing. To be handling a case which had apparently floored the Chief Justice was not so satisfactory as I had at first thought. I was standing where angels had feared to tread.

Next day, I sent for the dome-headed landlord, and again tried to reason with him. He sat before me coolly, hands folded like an old woman. Once again, I tried every argument I could think of, every appeal that might evoke response from even a single drop of mercy in his heart. But there was none, it seemed. Most of the time he said nothing. When I asked him a question he remained silent, leaving it to me to pursue another line of argument, his eyes looking always steadily a little below mine. Once or twice, turning his head very slightly towards the interpreter, he said quietly, his lips scarcely moving:

"I want them off."

He never once addressed me directly.

As the clock moved from the quarter to the half, I felt my whole body becoming cold with loathing for the man. What he wanted was simply power—power for its own sake—and he had got it on a tiny but absolute scale, power over everyone, from the Chief Justice down to the humblest squatter.

"People like you," I said at last, resignedly, "don't deserve to be alive. What you have done is inhuman, and I think I have every right to order you to take that wall down within a week from today."

He slowly turned his head away from me, dropping his eyelids slightly, his appearance in profile giving me his answer in silence:

"Order what you like. I know where I stand."

And suddenly I saw it.

116

The prim, cruel lips; the weak hands.

Brought up by amahs, I had said to myself, the instant I first saw him. Son of a third or fourth mother, I now mentally added. Brought up in a lonely house with high ceilings, perhaps; seldom seeing his father, and separated from his brothers who, the sons of other mothers, dwelt elsewhere. Brought up alone in a world of neglected women, telling him what to do and what not to do; and impuissant among them—desiring power, but never having any.

The wall *was* an act of revenge. But not against the sixteen shopkeepers. It was an act of revenge against those amahs and women of his youth, who had cared for him, but who (though he did not realize this) had brought him up to be a weakling, and whom he subconsciously hated.

He could probably have explained the wall in some strange way of his own. But it would not have been the real explanation. Of his real motive he was unaware, as would be my interpreter, as would be the actor and every other Chinese concerned with the wall. Freud was not born in China.

But there it was. The impression I had formed of his childhood might not be correct in every respect; but it was, I felt sure, as near to the truth as made no difference. Men seldom act without reason, even though it be a subconscious one.

And it was a relief to know that there *was* reason behind the building of the wall. I knew myself powerless before the man; but as he went away, coolly triumphant, I found I loathed him less.

Three days later, in connexion with something quite different, I was reading through the text of a standard Crown lease; and among the mass of small print, with no commas or semi-colons anywhere (why do lawyers make things so unnecessarily difficult?), my eye alighted on the word which had recently been so much on my mind—wall. Reading the immensely involved sentence a second time, it appeared that in the New Territories no one had the right to build a wall, even on his own land, without first obtaining a permit.

As will by now have become apparent, there were permits for nearly everything in the district. If someone had told me one needed a permit to sneeze, it would not have surprised me. The purpose of the permits was not revenue-raising; most of them cost next to nothing. They were part of the administration's armoury—weapons, by means of which we got things done the way we wanted them.

"For heaven's sake!" I exclaimed aloud. "I think we've got him!"

I rang through to the land officers.

"Find out if that man's got a permit for his wall, will you?"

"A *permit*, sir?" said an astonished voice.

Not even the land officers, it transpired, had realized that a permit was required for a wall. Neither, I could but presume, had the Chief Justice, or any of the lawyers. The Special Magistrate had, as it were, made a discovery.

Word was received the following day that the wall man did not have a permit. I sent for the land officers.

"I've already given that man verbally seven days' notice to pull his wall down. The notice expires on Wednesday morning. He won't pull it down, I'm quite sure; so I want you to make arrangements for it to be pulled down by ourselves on Wednesday afternoon."

They looked glum. Where was the money to come from?

It was the old song. There was no money anywhere in

our estimates for the enforcement of such orders as this. Everything in the district, when it came down to it, was done by bluff and permits.

"Surely the shopowners must know of a cheap contractor who can help them. I'm quite sure they'll be prepared to pay."

"One of them *is* a small contractor," said one of the land officers.

"Very good. Problem settled. Lay it on, and two of you go down there when the demolition takes place, so that it's all under your supervision. Take a few police constables as well. It adds tone."

And thus the wall came down.

The actor was in the office a couple of days after this, and looked in to see me.

"Well," I said cheerfully, "are you feeling happier?"

He grinned.

"Oh yes, we've all been much happier these few days. But"—he hesitated, his expression altering—"forgive me, sir, but I don't think this is the end of it. That man is very clever."

Sure enough, on the tenth day following, the landlord's contractor once more appeared on the scene with his men, and completely reconstructed the wall. And once again, no one resisted.

I sent for the dome-headed landlord.

"I understand you better now," I said to him. "You are not only inhuman, you are a fool. Don't you realize that we're going to pull that wall down again, and that we're going to pull it down again and again, however many times you try to rebuild it? Now, will you please get that into your head, and leave those poor people in peace!"

He made no reply, but from the side pocket of his long

gown he drew forth a small piece of paper, carefully unfolded it and laid it on the desk before me.

It was a wall permit, issued on behalf of the Director of Public Works. By an anomaly in the law, in the New Kowloon area both the Department of Public Works and the New Territories Administration had the right to issue permits, and our man knew it. The actor was right: he was very clever.

In cold fury I telephoned the official who had signed the permit, a European, and asked him what he thought he was doing interfering in a case that was before my court. To my increased fury, he was totally undisturbed. What was the use of bothering about all these people, he asked? They were only squatters, and squatters were a pain in the neck anyway. The man had every right to build a wall if he wanted to. If those people moved off his land, it might tidy the place up a bit. In any case, the entire area was scheduled for demolition, to make way for a new resettlement estate.

"In three or four years' time, maybe," I said. "What are these people going to do in the meantime?"

"God knows," the official replied. "I couldn't care less. They shouldn't be there."

It was, I reminded myself, a technician speaking, not an administrator; and technicians are practical and sane, administrators sentimental and mad. Like old age and youth, they never go together.

It was useless. The permit had been issued by a technician; and it is in the nature of the relationship between administrators and technicians that a technician will seldom, if ever, admit that he is in the wrong; to stick to his guns is the technician's only defence against being constantly overridden by the administrator, who in the last resort is the senior of the two. Furthermore, the gentleman seated before me had *paid* for that permit—paid more than the small sum stated on it. Somewhere along the line, 'black' money had changed hands. The piece of paper on my desk smelt of it.

Like Chinese salt fish, like French pedigree cheeses, corruption has an unmistakable smell. To pretend that any government in the world is free of it is foolishness. It is necessary, however, to recognize its fundamental law. Once 'black' money has changed hands, the direction of events has been set; and the most powerful autocrat will be unable to change it.

We had failed. Even were I to take the matter up personally with the Director of Public Works, whom I knew socially, his departmental officers would only procrastinate, lose the file, or some such thing, until, after a year or so, the appointment of an Arbitration Tribunal would give warning to all concerned that the days of that particular shanty town were numbered—to be replaced, admittedly, by something much better for everybody. And as the bulldozers moved in to do their work, the only serious obstacle they would meet—indeed, the only solid construction in the place—would be the wall.

I handed the permit back to the unsmiling man, and with a gesture indicated that he might go. I could not bring myself to speak to him. The very sight of him made me feel sick.

It was not the kind of case one could ever forget. But I was not thinking about it, thank heaven, when one day, looking up from a file, I found the actor seated before me. It was the first time I had seen him since.

"Oh!" I said sadly. "I'm so sorry!"

But he only smiled in a kindly way.

"Don't worry, sir. You tried your best for all of us. We know that." From his pocket he took out a small object, which he kept concealed in his hand. "We talked about it. And we want you to accept this. It's from us all."

He laid the object on the desk. Enclosed in a delicate little ivory container, it was an ivory seal with my Chinese name on it, carved by himself. Each one of the sixteen shopowners had contributed his share to this charming—and somehow strangely humbling—gift.

I tried to say something, but found I could not speak. Before I could recover myself, with a wave and a smile he had gone.

9

Mandamus

ADMITTEDLY, THE SPECIAL MAGISTRATE had had his failures —the wall case was one of them—but at the end of two years in office there was one point on which he felt he could certainly congratulate himself. He still knew nothing about law, and his ignorance of it had never made the slightest difference—or so it seemed to him.

Throughout two years, he had succeeded in not hearing a single case according to the common law. There had been one or two close moments, during which he feared he might be obliged to (and thus be revealed, as it were, nude), but he had developed a technique for dealing with people who insisted on a hearing in common law, and it always worked.

Whenever a complainant opted for the common law, as opposed to Chinese law and custom, it was because he believed he would score an advantage by it. A gentle hint from the Special Magistrate on this point, and the defendant would instantly opt for Chinese law and custom, thus creating a difference which could be reconciled only by the Special Magistrate deciding, very correctly, in favour of the defendant. This technique had proved cast-iron.

Once embarked on Chinese law and custom, which was simpler and more informal, there was a fair likelihood of the Special Magistrate being able to grasp what a case was about, which under the common law it was useless to pretend there would be.

The Special Magistrate, celebrating the start of his third year in office, had been expatiating at a Chinese dinner on his prowess in having had nothing to do with the common law; matters were changed the next morning when, the warming fumes of the dinner still upon him, he answered the telephone.

The caller was a leading European barrister-at-law, considered a formidable figure by many government officials, since he was, in addition, a leading Hongkong politician, and an outspoken critic of government shortcomings.

It so happened, however, that he and the Special Magistrate were personal friends. They saw a good deal of each other, too, on an official basis, since the barrister owned one of the largest farms in the district, where he did all the classically correct things, such as improving stock and encouraging arboriculture. Thinking he had rung up on some matter concerned with the farm, the Special Magistrate had mentally settled himself down to a pleasant conversation, when to his consternation the barrister said:

"You have a case in your office concerning a man called Lu."

"Have we?" I replied nonchalantly—but I didn't like the sound of it; I knew what my friend was like when he got his teeth into something.

"Yes. You may not know it, but you have," he answered, in a tone which chided me with 'the law's delays, the insolence of office'. "He's a client of mine in another matter. He's complained to me that you've kept his case pending a very long time."

"Really? What's the case about?"

"He's trying to evict a man who he says is cultivating some fields of his illegally."

"Oh! *That* case!" I said. "I know it."

"Have you given a date for a hearing?" he pursued.

"No, I shouldn't think so," I replied, this time with genuine nonchalance.

"Well, when are you going to give one?"

"I haven't any idea."

My friend's voice rose.

"But he says you've already kept the case pending more than five months."

"Is it as long as that? It may be."

"Austin," he said sternly, "are you, or are you not, going to hear that case?"

"Not if I can help it. You know, cases of that kind are a complete waste of time."

At the other end of the line, I could feel him draw himself up.

"Forgive me for saying so," he said, with studied politeness, "but it surely isn't your business to say whether or not a case is a waste of time."

"No," I admitted, "I don't suppose it is. But this one, I can assure you, is."

I had not realized I had delayed a hearing quite so long as five months, but I certainly had delayed it, and deliberately, hoping that the complainant would grow tired of waiting, and resort to some better way of settling it.

Curiously enough, long before being posted to the district, I had come across several similar cases; in the office I had tried to settle several more; and now there was this one. Basically, they were all of them the same.

When the Japanese invaded Hongkong in 1941, many members of wealthy Chinese families, rightly foreseeing that they ran the risk of being dubbed running-dogs of the British and having their homes requisitioned by the Japanese military, and also foreseeing that, with international shipping at a standstill, Hongkong faced a serious food shortage, quietly removed themselves to their ancestral villages in China, where they could lie low, and where, despite uncomfortable living conditions, there would at least be enough to eat.

These departures were usually made in a hurry, and matters had to be disposed of rapidly. In the case of the Lu family, one of the family retainers, a young man aged about twenty-two, and who was not in such danger from the Japanese as were his employers, asked at the last moment if he could help the family, and himself, by staying behind and farming two large fields that the family owned, on the lower slopes of Kowloon Peak in the hills terminating the Kowloon urban area. The family agreed and departed.

When they returned to Hongkong four years later, the man was still farming the fields. But when he came to see the family, expecting to be re-employed by them, he found them very busy re-starting their commercial affairs, and unable to give him much attention.

Though the family did not say so, they did not want to re-engage him. He was no longer the meek young man who would do everything he was told, and keep awake all hours. He was a self-reliant cultivator with his own ideas—not the type of person the family was looking for. Taking the line of least resistance, Mrs. Lu got rid of him by telling him he could go on cultivating the fields.

Ten years passed, during which land values and rents rose steadily. Meanwhile, the cultivator continued on the two fields, paying no rent.

Then, unexpectedly, Mr. Lu received a handsome offer

from a company which wished to buy (but was also prepared to rent) the fields, for growing special grass for cattle-fodder. The company had taken a lease, for the same purpose, of a large area of Crown land, in the middle of which the two fields were situated. It was important to the company to obtain possession of the fields, since this would make the scheme more economical. Commercially, Mr. Lu was on a good wicket.

The cultivator, however, now a married man with children, refused to vacate the fields, saying the Lu family had given him permission to farm them indefinitely. There was no written agreement of any kind between the family and their ex-retainer; and the family were thus caught, victims of their own negligence.

This was the reason why I said the case was a waste of time. In court, each of the parties would be able to say whatever they liked, and claim they spoke the truth. But, in fact, there would be no proof of anything.

In my view, there was only one way of settling the matter; and I had delayed in the hope that Mr. Lu might realize what this was, without my having to tell him. As a boy, the cultivator had been their family retainer, and the son of one; and if they now wished him to quit their land, it was up to them to set him up in a small business somewhere, or make him some equally suitable present. They had apparently not considered doing this. Instead, they had brought what I considered a ridiculous suit, to waste the time of our office.

But my barrister friend was not going to allow me to get away with it.

"Well then, may I ask you," he said, "to fix a date *now* for a hearing."

"I can assure you, it's no use," I replied. "Your client will get nowhere."

I could almost see him raising his eyes to the ceiling, and feel him gripping the telephone harder.

"Austin, you are a *magistrate*," he said firmly, his patience distinctly ebbing. "It is not your business to pass judgment on cases without hearing them."

"Yes, but you see, we know about the case, and we *know* it's hopeless."

There was a pause.

"Look here, old boy, I'm very sorry to have to say this," he said slowly, "but I'm quite serious. If you don't fix a date for a hearing here and now, I warn you that I shall be obliged to apply for a writ of *Mandamus* against you."

"*Mandamus?*" I exclaimed. "What on earth's that?"

He coughed slightly, in a most legal manner.

"By a writ of *Mandamus*, filed on behalf of my client in the Supreme Court, we can *demand* that you, as a magistrate, shall hear a case."

"How terrible!" I said. "I never knew there *was* such a law. Well, if you insist, I suppose I shall have to hear it. But your client's making a great mistake, if I may say so. He doesn't understand the New Territories. It's no use these urban people coming into this office and insisting, as he has, that we hear a suit of this kind according to the common law." (It was essential to get this point tidied up.) "The common law is useless in a dispute of this kind, in my opinion."

"*Please*," my friend begged, "please may I remind you that, if a litigant requests you to hear a case under the common law, *you hear it under the common law!*"

It meant the cast-iron move.

"Yes," I said, "but what about the cultivator? Supposing he doesn't agree?"

"The cultivator, I understand, does agree. He, too, wishes the case to be heard under the common law."

"Oh!" I gasped.

With a sinking feeling in the pit of my stomach, I leaned for my diary and fixed a date.

"Po Wah," I said, as I finally put the telephone down, "I know it's not very ethical, but ask Mr. Lo to call up that cultivator, and try to convince him he's making a mistake—which he is—in not having his case heard according to Chinese law and custom."

After two entire years of the neatest evasion, *surely* the ineluctable moment could not have come when I should be faced with *two* parties demanding the common law. It was too dreadful to contemplate. If my complete ignorance of the law was discovered, I might even have to resign.

Though the government had unintentionally made a mistake in appointing me to a post bearing magisterial functions, they could hardly be expected to say much in my defence, should I put them publicly to shame. I should at least have *tried* to study law.

But the ineluctable moment had come. Mr. Lo, who by this time was well aware of my legal—and other—shortcomings, and who also shared my view that Chinese cases were settled far more equitably by Chinese methods than by British ones, told me afterwards that he did everything he could to make the cultivator change his mind, but he would not.

When the day came, I arrived in my office to find that the staff, too, were aware that this was an occasion of some importance. All files had been removed from my desk; the glass on top had been cleaned, fresh blotting paper laid out, and a sheaf of paper provided, since everything said would have to be written down. Chairs had been arranged for the rival parties, with additional chairs for the lawyers who were expected also to be present. It all looked horribly solemn, and I felt the situation was beyond me. I was not this kind of magistrate.

I sat down at my desk. It was a very warm day, but I felt cold and dreadful.

Mr. Lo came in, carrying a Bible.

"What on earth are you doing with that?" I asked.

He looked very serious. All the proceedings, he explained, had to be under oath.

Mentally I groaned. The intrusion of oaths, in my view, demonstrated a total misapprehension of what a Chinese court is. Naturally, in a Chinese court, no one is expected to tell the truth, and few ever do. Perjury is a word all but untranslatable into Chinese. In every suit it could confidently be assumed that everyone would tell lies. It was the magistrate's duty to sift the lies and, by instinct, work his way through them to the correct decision. As a senior Chinese colleague of mine in the Hongkong administration, for many years a magistrate himself, once wisely said to me, "No Chinese is going to tell the truth unless he can see some advantage in doing so. Why should he? Truth is private property."

It was a statement with which I entirely agreed. The only valid oath I knew of in a Chinese court was when someone swore he was telling the truth, and the other party challenged him to kill a cock in a temple to prove it. To kill a cock in such circumstances was something which very few would dare do, unless what they had maintained was indeed true.

But statements made on oath in this manner normally occurred at the end of an otherwise insoluble dispute, not at the beginning. Had we insisted on every case beginning with people taking valid Chinese oaths, the place would have been in a terrible mess.

It will be observed to what degree two years in the district had caused my mental processes to change. Admittedly, I had had no experience of the law in England or anywhere else; all I knew of that kind of law was what I had seen in the movies. But as its trappings were introduced into my office, I felt instantly hostile—even to the Bible. What chiefly upset me, I think, was that, realizing that oaths of this kind would make no difference to the degree of untruth that came into the court, the taking of them at once clothed the proceedings in a veil of hypocrisy.

Viewed historically, oaths on the Bible were admittedly a considerable improvement on ordeal by fire. But this was Anglo-Saxon history, not Chinese. In this entirely Chinese situation, it would have been greatly preferable, in my view, for everybody to have been allowed to tell lies in their usual honest and straightforward fashion.

The parties were ushered in and took their places. Mr. Lu was legally represented; the cultivator was not.

In the New Territories, a magistrate has the right to refuse to hear lawyers. There is a tendency in nearly every proceeding for the Magistrate to be a kind of counsel for the defence—anyway, to have to prompt the defendant from time to time—and it seemed to me that this situation would be even more pronounced with a lawyer conducting the case for the other side. I also had in mind what Mr. Lu might be going to say afterwards to my barrister friend—perhaps, that I had unduly helped the defendant, or twisted the truth?—accusations which, friend or no friend, could put me in serious trouble with the government. I declined to hear lawyers.

Mr. Lu had not expected this, and was disconcerted. He held a whispered discussion with his lawyer. Might his lawyer remain and listen? Certainly he might. The lawyer took a seat at the rear, and we began.

Mr. Lu, evidently a Christian, took the usual oath on the Bible, and proceeded to make his statement. Because I had to write it all down, it went at a snail's pace, and my resentment of the entire business mounted. There we were, with a mass of urgent and more useful work awaiting attention, stuck for hours recording wearisome facts, every one of which was already known to us. It was, as I had told the barrister, an utter waste of time.

One fact, however, was new—though it was not a fact which could be written down. The cultivator, when I had time to have a good look at him, appeared to be a thoroughly unpleasant character. He had a low, ribbed forehead; moody, calculating eyes and a wide mouth, at both sides of which ran downward-sloping lines of contempt.

He would, I judged, be a man of few friends. He was as hard as nails, broad-boned and strong, and had clearly come in a bolstered-up mood, in which he would not be prepared to budge an inch. As he first came into the room, there was something about him that resembled an actor assuming his stated rôle. Though he made not the slightest movement as he sat before me, he was all gesture.

Mr. Lu, on the other hand, quietly attired in a well-tailored European suit, was a reasonable person, evidently a man of some experience, and, it was clear, born with money. He obviously belonged to a vintage Hongkong Chinese family; one could almost have told which road he lived in, on what level of Victoria Peak. He had insisted on the case being heard according to the common law, probably because, like his father and grandfather before him, he had respect for British justice, and believed he was going about things the proper way.

He was not; but with a writ of *Mandamus* hanging over my head there was nothing I could do about it.

Like many rich people he was unaccustomed to unpleasant confrontations, and was nervous, both with me and with the cultivator, at whom he did not once look. He had not expected to find himself so exposed, as people always were in my little court. It occurred to me that he might even be wondering whether he had not made a mistake in taking the advice of his lawyers.

The atmosphere in the room was totally different from how it usually was. I was not a Chinese magistrate today. Today I was a British magistrate, and being extremely unsure of myself in this capacity, I was defensively giving away nothing. A crisp word here, a curt question there; no more. Writing fast, out of the corner of my eye I could see Mr. Lu calculating, as he watched me, that he had run up against a pretty cold fish.

Despite his nerves, he made a good, clear statement, however, after which we passed to the cultivator. With him, Mr. Lo did not use the Bible. Instead, he administered a Chinese oath, which served to re-awaken my hostility to this form of proceeding. It was evidently a standard form of oath, but where it originated, goodness knows. It was in archaic British Chinese, if such a thing is imaginable. To me it meant nothing at all. Neither, it was plain, did it to the cultivator, who only with some difficulty managed to get his tongue round it. This formality completed, we carried on.

From the first words he uttered, the cultivator was

truculent. Several times he had to be reminded to give facts, not opinions. Before very long I felt I understood exactly why Mrs. Lu had got rid of him, in the way she had, in 1945. She had almost certainly been afraid of him.

The situation in law, so far as I could see, was that, never having paid rent, the cultivator was in the position of being a licensee, i.e. he had been given licence by Mrs. Lu to occupy the fields, licence which could technically be revoked at will. There remained, however, the custom of the country, which was that no one should be required to vacate a field on which there were standing crops. The fields at present were fully planted with young cabbages.

Having taken down the cultivator's statement, I asked Mr. Lu if he wished to say anything. He merely reminded me that he had given the defendant notice to quit nearly six months ago. It was when the latter had refused to receive the written notice that Mr. Lu had brought the case to us.

He did not have to say more. Cabbages do not take that time to grow. What had happened was that, within the past few months, the cultivator had sold one crop and planted another. Only a few weeks ago, Mr. Lu stated further, the man had built a pigstye beside the fairly substantial wooden hut he had in the middle of the fields, and installed eight pigs.

To my ears, there was something odd about this. I asked the cultivator if it was true he had pigs on the land.

Yes, it was. He had permission to be on the land, and could do what he liked.

"Eight pigs?" I queried. "You mean, you bought a sow, and it had seven piglets?"

No. He had bought eight pigs approaching maturity.

"That was rather an expensive proposition, wasn't it?"

This riled him, and he made what I considered to be an error. He said sullenly:

"They can't get me off my fields. I've been paying them rent for ten years."

"You've been paying rent?" I asked rapidly.

"Yes."

"Does the complainant give you rent receipts?"

"Yes."

"Can you produce one?"

"No. I throw them away."

"When did you last pay rent?"

"Six months ago."

He was lying, of course. But it was only fair to warn him that his lie had wrecked his case.

"Think carefully," I said to him quietly. "Are you quite sure you have been paying rent?"

He was quite sure.

"And you have not paid for six months?"

Correct.

"Then, as I see it, by withholding payment of rent, you have accepted the complainant's notice to quit, and must so quit."

The copy of the letter asking him to vacate the fields, and which Mr. Lu claimed the defendant had refused to receive, was again produced. It gave him six months in which to move, a period which was due to expire in ten days.

I found that the complainant had duly and properly given the defendant notice to quit, and ordered that the latter remove himself and his effects from the fields within ten days, warning him that failure to do so would result in his hut, pigs, and other possessions being removed by officers of the law and confiscated.

I felt sick and disgusted with myself.

They had not departed more than five minutes when the second of my land officers came in. He was a young Portuguese, a cheerful, lively person, who kept his ear to the ground.

"You know that man's a communist, sir, don't you?" he said genially.

"Which man?"

"That cultivator you had in here just now. I understand he has communist support."

I lean back in my chair. "I see!" I murmured.

All the odd features of the hearing suddenly made sense. Those pigs: that man could not possibly have paid for them himself; they had been borrowed from someone, and this had been organized for him. His truculence, too; that bolstered-up attitude of his. It had been inspired by others around him. And his lie about paying rent had been made with a deliberate intention. The communists wished to be certain I would give the order I had. It was for this reason they had told the cultivator to insist on the common law.

Though Mr. Lu and his legal advisers were obviously unaware of it, the thing was a deliberately rigged communist plot to create a public incident; and I had unsuspectingly done exactly what was required of me.

Sure enough, the following morning, a short report of the case appeared in both the leading communist newspapers. The reports described the hardships of a poor and industrious tiller of the soil, persecuted by a rich and evil landlord. No special prominence was given to it; each report was quite far down the page. But it was from such modest beginnings that large troubles grew.

The six-month period expired, and the cultivator did not

move. Henry, my Portuguese land officer, even reported that he thought there were now nine pigs.

The office having no actual power to enforce anything, I telephoned the Supreme Court, and arranged with the Chief Bailiff for the removal of the cultivator's property.

"How many men will be needed?" the Chief Bailiff, a European, inquired.

Being unfamiliar with bailiffs and their work-speeds, I was at a loss.

"Well, just what is there to be removed?" he asked.

"A fair-sized wooden dwelling-hut and toolshed, a pig-stye, nine pigs, and about three acres of cabbages."

"I beg your pardon?" he said, with some consternation.

I repeated the list. He said he thought three men would be enough. An exact day and hour were fixed.

In the mysterious way they always did, the communists quickly learned of this day and hour. Mr. Lo informed me that we might expect a sizeable number of fellow-cultivators to assemble at that time, and offer resistance to the bailiffs. I telephoned the police.

We so seldom telephoned the police—using Chinese law and custom we rarely needed their services—that the divisional superintendent did me the courtesy of coming round to see me personally. He was a man I had known since my earliest days in Hongkong, a fluent Chinese speaker, able to read Chinese with ease, and a person with a sensitive feel for a political situation.

I explained the case, and said I was expecting trouble.

"How many cultivators d'you think will turn up?" he asked.

"About eighty, I'm told, but that's probably exaggerated."

"I don't think so. Have you been watching the Chinese press?"

He explained that, although the communist newspapers had made no further direct reference to the case, each day articles on landlordism had been appearing, which he now realized, he said, were innuendo references to Mr. Lu and the cultivator, and indicated that things were hotting up.

It had all the makings of a thoroughly ugly incident, as well as being an absurd one. The prospect of a posse of European bailiffs uprooting Chinese cabbages gave the situation a rare charm, but not if the bailiffs were to be surrounded, as seemed likely, by a struggling mass of farmers and uniformed police. Unlike the case of the watercress beds, where we were tidily tucked away on a fairly remote island, these fields were highly accessible, less than fifteen minutes by car from Kowloon, and situated next to a main road. Communist press photographers would certainly be there, Peking Radio would have the story within hours, and wherever the photographs appeared, in no matter what country, they would throw an extremely unfavourable light on the conduct of the Hongkong Government.

However, just that morning I had had an unexpected call from that important, but seldom seen functionary, the permit clerk, who had taken the liberty, as he had put it, of bringing me a small piece of information which he thought might interest me. It had. I did not divulge any of this to the superintendent of police, because the information was something that had to be kept closely up my sleeve.

"The way I see this thing is like this," I said, after we had mutually assessed matters. "There is still just a chance that I may be able to settle this case satisfactorily, without having to throw the man off the land. But it's only just a chance, and it may not succeed. I'm sure you agree that it's undesirable to have police actually on the site when the bailiffs arrive. At the same time, if my plan fails, we shall obviously need police help, and quickly. Would it be possible to have the police concealed behind the hills around the site and for them to get there inconspicuously, giving no indication that we're in the least worried about the case, or expecting trouble?"

"Easily," he replied. He liked the idea.

"Very well. I'll be at the site myself. Tell the officer in charge to have field glasses, and to watch me carefully. If my plan fails, and we need police help, I'll light a cigar. After that, I leave the rest to you."

"How many men d'you think you need?"

"After what you say about the press, I should say about two hundred."

"We'll make it four hundred," he said crisply. He was a most reassuring person to have around.

When he had gone, I sent for Mr. Lo.

"Telephone Mr. Lu, will you please, and tell him, with my compliments, that I require him to be at the site with me when the bailiffs come. He and his lawyers have caused all this trouble, and I want him to witness the consequences."

Mr. Lo looked doubtful.

"I don't think he'll agree to come, sir. He'll be too frightened they might attack him."

"If that's his answer when you speak to him, tell him, again with my compliments, that if he doesn't come of his own volition, he will be arrested and brought. He has got to be there."

Mr. Lu, it was later reported, reluctantly agreed to come.

To my everlasting regret, when the day came, I missed the scene at the fields. Fifteen minutes before I was due to leave, I was handed a complicated land problem, on which the Secretariat required an immediate answer, and was confined to the office for the rest of the afternoon.

I sent for Henry. Among other things, Henry was the colony's champion marksman, and he enjoyed anything that relished of an adventure.

"You'll have to take my place at this communist cultivator business," I told him. "Have you a cigar?"

He smirked.

"I don't smoke, sir."

"Well, this afternoon you may have to. Take one of mine."

He looked dubiously at the sealed end of it.

"You bite that bit off," I explained. "Here, let me do it for you." I cut it with a penknife.

"I shall probably be sick," he murmured.

"Can't be helped," I replied, and telephoned the police to warn them of the change in personnel.

"What do I have to do, sir?" asked Henry, his mystification increasing.

"Just this," I said, "and remember every detail carefully.

"There'll probably be quite a large crowd up there when you arrive. Stand where you can be seen clearly from all directions. When the bailiffs come, tell them to do nothing until you give them the go-ahead. Mr. Lu will be there—and if he isn't, you must drive at once to the nearest telephone, and let me know. But I think he will be there. Let the crowd clearly see who are the men who are going to uproot the cabbages—that's to say, the bailiffs—and let there be no doubt in anyone's mind that you are just about to give them the order to begin. There'll be a hostile reaction; it'll probably be pretty nasty. Play it for a moment or two. Let Mr. Lu see it and feel it.

"Then I want you to tell him something. Say that you have been authorized by me to tell him that if, tomorrow morning, Chou En-lai's office telephones the British Embassy in Peking, and there's an international shindy, it will be entirely Mr. Lu's fault. You will also tell him that I shall ensure that this detail is properly understood by the public of Hongkong. Get it?"

Henry grinned and nodded. It was just his line of country.

"Next, I want you to ask Mr. Lu a question. Again, tell him you are asking this question on my authority. If I agree to cancel the entire proceedings of this case as heard under the common law, will he agree to allow me to deal with it according to Chinese law and custom?

"Give him time to think. You can warn him it's a grave decision. If he refuses, stand quite prominently apart from the other people, and light the cigar—d'you carry matches?"

"No, sir."

"Well, take these. Lighting the cigar is the signal for the police, hidden behind the surrounding hills, to descend from all sides, and surround the fields. Goodness knows what will happen then—you'd better tell Lu to get into his car and drive like hell. Apart from that, don't do anything until the police officer in charge tells you he's ready. Then the bailiffs can go in and start their work."

Henry, throughout this, had been looking more and more jubilant. Undiscovered lacunae in his sense of responsibility had unexpectedly surfaced. Finally, his face fell, and in an almost agonized tone of disappointment, he asked:

"But, what if he agrees, sir?"

I withdrew slightly on the back legs of my chair.

"If he agrees, just tell them they can all go home, including the bailiffs."

Henry looked nonplussed.

"Just go home?"

"Yes. You too. Only come and see me first."

"But what about Mr. Lu? Won't you want to see him?"

"No," I said casually, "I don't think so."

Henry crooked his bronzed head slightly and gave me a cagey look.

"What are you going to do, sir?" he inquired, with a knowing glint in his eye.

"Never you mind," I replied. "Let's just see what happens next."

With a delightful air of expectancy, he strode out of the room, blowing out imaginary smoke, the cigar held to his lips.

"For goodness' sake," I cried in alarm, "don't do that!"

At the door he paused, and looking back with a cat-like grin, said:

"Don't worry, sir. I was only imitating you."

I buried myself in the file the Secretariat was asking for.

When, after thirty minutes, there was no call from Henry, I presumed that Mr. Lu had reached the site. With my mind only half on it, I dictated a long—and probably rather badly thought out—memorandum on the land problem. Finally, towards closing time, Henry returned.

"Phew!" he exclaimed, as he walked in, wiping imaginary sweat from his brow. "That was quite an event!"

"What happened?" I asked quietly. The staff always knew when I was keenly interested or involved in anything. On my side, it meant I felt I had to do my utmost not to show it.

As Henry explained it, he reached the fields to find, in

142

his estimation, upward of nine hundred men, standing in a single, unbroken line around the entire boundary of the fields. As anticipated, press and cameras were there, not overtly communists (they seldom were), but engaged by them. The bailiffs, as I could have sworn they would, arrived in a little British car, absurdly unimposing, and wearing clothes suggesting that they were looking forward to a pleasant, rustic afternoon.

That they had chosen the afternoon as being a suitable time to come was a feature that added charm to their already charming participation. Calculating, firstly, closing time for work, and secondly, sundown, they were left (after being warned by Henry to do nothing until told) to study how much three men can do in three hours on three acres of cabbages, not to mention the house and pigs.

There was also the cultivator to be reckoned with. His fields surrounded by his nine hundred supporters, he was in his hut (he lived there alone), from which from time to time he emerged holding a cooking pot, leaving no one in reasonable doubt that he was preparing his evening meal. Communist art has always stuck closely to realism.

"Well, go on, Henry! What did you do?" I asked, beginning to lose patience.

"I did what you said, sir," he replied.

"Well, tell me! What happened?"

Without a word, he laid the cigar on my desk. It was unsmoked.

"Good," I murmured. "What did Mr. Lu say?"

Henry raised his eyebrows, and made a grimace.

"He was in rather a state," he said.

"I'm sure he was, Henry. But what did he *say*?" I demanded impatiently.

Imitating Mr. Lu, Henry fluttered his hands in the air.

143

"He said, 'Anything the Li Man Fu wants! Anything the Li Man Fu wants!'"

"Very satisfactory, Henry," I said quietly, concealing my relief. "And so, you all got into your cars, and went home?"

"Yes, sir."

"Leaving the nine hundred still standing there, and without a word of explanation to them?"

"Of course, sir!"

I leaned on my desk, and nodded with satisfaction.

"Bless you, Henry! Just what I wanted."

What a perfect anticlimax for them!

"But, sir, Mr. Lu wanted to come and see you. He wanted to fix a date for the new hearing," Henry went on, rather anxiously.

"Maybe. Did you get him to go home?"

"With difficulty, yes."

"Good. Ask the permit clerk to come and see me, would you."

Still mystified, he went; and a moment later, the permit clerk came in.

Poor fellow, he was about the only member of the staff who had no opportunity to enjoy the sun and the country air. He always looked as white as a sheet.

"You remember," I said to him, "telling me the other day about that cultivator's wife having a vegetable stall in some quite different part of the district—was it Tsuen Wan?"

He nodded in silent expectation.

"Send her a registered letter immediately, giving her seven days' notice of cancellation of her stall licence."

He nodded again, and made for the door.

"And, Ah Lau," I added—he paused an instant—"thank you."

Four days later, from Mr. Lu's fields, the dwelling-hut, the toolshed, the pigstye, the pigs, the cultivator, had gone. A token number of cabbages had been pulled up, the rest left to rot.

A week or so later, we noticed that the cattle-fodder company had taken over.

It was quicker than I had expected. I had often wondered why the cultivator lived in the hut alone. Unexpectedly, we had tapped his main source of income.

Some months afterwards, I happened to see Mr. Lu at a large reception in the city. He avoided me, and I sensed he was embarrassed. Seeking him out, I broke the ice and asked him if he was satisfied. It appeared he was, and he was very friendly. We discussed various commonplaces until, with a sudden intake of breath, he pounced the question:

"How did you do it?"

"By Chinese law and custom," I replied serenely. "Oblige me by telling your legal representatives."

It would hardly have been seemly, after all, to have explained to him that, like nearly everything else in the district, the matter had been settled by bluff and permits.

Because, of course, once the cultivator was off Mr. Lu's land, the cultivator's wife's vegetable stall licence was *not* cancelled.

There is a postscript to this story, which, on the plane of human relations, it gives me pleasure to recall. A few weeks later, we were engaged in moving several hundred squatters to a new site, which would again be only temporary for them, but which would at least keep them going for a year or so, until permanent accommodation could be built. Whom should we find among them but the very same cultivator, who, to our surprise, gave complete co-operation to my field staff, thereby giving the lead to his neighbours, resulting in the most smoothly-conducted squatter clearance ever conducted during my time.

In appreciation, we put him at the top of the list of those scheduled to receive a free grant of pedigree pigs; and I understand he did well with them. It was the small postscripts, such as this, which always gave the Special Magistrate much happiness.

An Island of Buddhist Perfection

OPINIONS DIFFER on how the giant African snail reached Hongkong. Certainly it was not smuggled there in a strip of bamboo.

Since it was in 1945 that the animal was first noted in large numbers, many have blamed its arrival on the Japanese, claiming that the snail reached Hongkong in the insufficiently cleaned holds of Japanese ships during the war.

It is difficult to see how this can be correct, however, if the snail came from Africa, since, during the war, Japanese ships had no access to African ports—unless, of course, the snail is not African, which is possible.

Other learned opinion states that the snail came from Taiwan, and again blame the Japanese for its presence in Hongkong.

Amid all the argument there is one point of certainty. The giant African snail may or may not be African, but it is assuredly a giant. Its effect on gardens and all forms of edible vegetation is lethal. During the winter the snails completely disappear. But with the warmth and humidity of spring and summer, huge armadas of them advance majestically, and with remarkable speed, upon all cultivated matter, devouring all before them, leaving in their tracks a mucus-like excretion which stifles any shoot of edible life the animal may have missed. Its shell mottled brown and yellow, and its skin a grey-tinted beige, the giant African snail is undeniably a noble and imposing creature. But it is a scourge of the countryside.

Its reproductive capacity is enormous. On the small island where, during these years as magistrate, I resided for part of each week, in the early summer (normally the wettest time of year) there must have been literally millions of them cruising around. They seemed to come from nowhere, and by instinct they moved towards any place, however remote of access, where there was cultivation.

My small garden, situated on a hill, seemed to be a kind of route for the snails, as, having eaten all my seedlings, they headed down towards a fertile area of vegetable fields some 130 feet below.

In every farm and garden, each morning started with a slaughter of snails. By noon, dead piles of them were a feature of every field. And next day it was the same all over again. In my garden—less than a ¼ acre—we killed a minimum of a hundred per morning; and there were lesser slaughterings in the afternoon and evening. Furthermore, they had to be crushed, a messy business, but there was no other way of killing them.

Chinese, with their innate sense of minding their own business, seldom killed the snails when they came across them on public paths, or on someone else's land, though on their own fields, or in their own gardens, they gave the creatures no mercy. I killed snails wherever I saw them and encouraged others to do the same.

I remember one morning when, having come in from the island very early, I was crossing in the public ferry from Hongkong to Kowloon, when by chance I found myself seated next to the abbot of a Buddhist monastery. With the aid of the Chinese friend I was with, I was exchanging pleasantries with the abbot when, glancing down, I realized the soles of my shoes were a sludgy mass of dead snailflesh. Without thinking what I was doing, with a grimace I showed my sole to the abbot, and said what a pest the snails were when you lived in the country.

Diplomatically, he did his best not to show it; but I could see he was very shocked; and it reminded me of the Buddha's sacred injunction: 'And for pity's sake, do not kill, lest ye harm some tiny creature on the upward path.'

"Nevertheless, Venerable One," I said in self-defence, "one has to draw the line somewhere. If we allowed these pestilential creatures to live, there would be no vegetables to eat."

Buddhists being vegetarians, I trusted he took the point.

The monk in question—the Very Venerable Sik Kam Moon, Abbot of the Monastery of the Exalted Eastern Gem—was a fairly frequent caller at the office.

He was all curves. The scrupulously shaven dome of his head was a curve, as were his cheeks and double chin. His figure was all curves; the folds of his robes hung in curves; from his waist, his prayer-beads fell in a curve.

And with this, he was all golden. His well-nourished skin was golden; his robes were a mellow gold; his prayer-beads were golden brown; and, as the completing touch, his name—Kam Moon—meant Overflow of Gold.

Needless to say, with such an abbot in charge of its affairs, the Monastery of the Exalted Eastern Gem was very rich.

How much the Very Venerable Overflow of Gold knew about Buddhism I never discovered. Not very much, I suspect. To me—and even more so to the office staff—he appeared to be as his name suggested, a business man, but a robed and vegetarian one. In addition, he was a crafty business man—at least, in the staff's opinion—and had on several occasions played tricks on the office.

In the West there still exists a widespread misconception that China is—or was, prior to communism—a Buddhist country.

It is true that for several hundred years, during the first Christian millennium, Buddhism enjoyed a court vogue in China, and many educated people became Buddhist. It could also be said that various Buddhist concepts took root among Chinese ideas, though even here, close examination reveals that some of these concepts are ancient Chinese, merely coated with a Buddhist gloss.

But Buddhism, with its fundamental tenet that this is a world of imperfection, never became a popular religion among the great mass of the Chinese people. The pessimism that underlies it inhibited any enduring appeal to a people for whom life and this world are essentially good, and to be enjoyed. At the beginning of this century, it is doubtful whether more than 7 per cent of China's population were practising Buddhists.

How the misconception grew abroad that China is a Buddhist country can only be deduced; but I suspect the Chinese were themselves partly responsible for it.

When the first Chinese started going abroad to Western countries, inevitably one of the first questions they were asked was, 'What is your religion?' But when, having first found out what Westerners meant by the word religion, they gave the correct answer, which is 'None', they were disconcerted to find this received with raised eyebrows, and the conclusion, 'Oh, so you're an atheist.'

To be an atheist, as they then learned, was a social stigma in the West. In addition, the Western conclusion was faulty, because although (apart from certain minority groups, such as the Buddhists and the Muslims) China has no religion in the Western sense, Chinese are not atheists in the Western sense either. They are far more conscious than are most Westerners of a spirit world; they accept, as a matter of course, that there is some kind of existence beyond death; and they are aware of invisible influences for good and evil.

Where they differ from the West—and from India—is that they do not trouble to probe into, or attempt to analyze, such matters too deeply, believing this to be morbid and profitless. To a traditionally educated Chinese scholar, the practice of religion in the Western sense indicates a species of neurosis and is considered unhealthy. Life, in such a view, should be seen as it is, without the bias which inevitably comes as an outcome of convictions based on speculation.

So how was the Chinese to reply to his Western interlocutor? If he replied that his religion was Confucianism, and was then asked to explain what this was, it provoked the reply, 'That's not a religion; it's a set of behaviour patterns.' It was no use saying he was a Taoist, because no one had ever heard of that, and would never understand it anyway. But Westerners had heard of the Buddha, and he was deemed respectable. Thus, when greeted with, 'You're from China? Ah, then you're a Buddhist!' the Chinese visitor, with an inward sigh of despair, gave up and said 'Yes.'

One of the most maddening remarks which Westerners make on the subject of the Orient, is that Oriental people are tricky to deal with, because they always give you the answer you want to hear. The foregoing hypothetical instance of the Chinese explaining what his religion is will perhaps help to clarify why this is so often seemingly so. As with the earlier instance about the Orient valuing life cheap, one cannot in polite society reply to a brief question by delivering a three-hour lecture. Yet a three-hour lecture is often what is needed before East and West can understand each other on even the simplest questions.

But, to continue, while not probing too deeply into what the West would call religious matters, neither do the Chinese exclude religious ideas. Anathema, in the Catholic sense, is unknown in Chinese tradition. The traditional Chinese approach to religious ideas, in fact, could perhaps be described as a negative eclecticism. And Buddhism, while having relatively few full adherents, found a place among many more millions of Chinese than strictly adhered to it, due to one particular matter. It became associated with death.

On first arrival in China, one of the baffling discoveries to be made—after the initial discovery that China is not Buddhist—is that (but not, of course, under communism) an enormous number of non-Buddhist families employ Buddhist priests to come to their homes to chant prayers after a death, and pay them large sums for doing so. Even those who pay the money will seldom swear they believe in the efficacy of the prayers, and will do all the traditional non-Buddhist things as well, such as burning large quantities of hell money, paper houses and whatnot, for the use of the deceased.

But there it is. On such occasions, Buddhism is used as an alternative other-world insurance policy, just in case there's something in it. It is similar to backing two horses in the same race.

Death and land transactions were Overflow of Gold's most lucrative sources of income on behalf of his monastery, but it was concerned with death that he brought off his major *coup* where my office was concerned.

The proliferation of graves is something which in South China has to be resisted with great firmness, if much good land, valuable for agriculture or housing development, is not to be wasted by becoming virtually private cemeteries. In Kwangtung province, the wastage of good land on private graves, scattered in every conceivable part of the countryside, was formidable; and one of Chairman Mao Tse-tung's first orders on assuming power was that any grave sited in an unsuitable spot, and more than five years old, should be dug up. The tenacity of the Chinese on this subject is shown by the frequency of newspaper references to graves in China, indicating that even after eighteen years of communist rule, there are many areas in which this order of Chairman Mao's has not been obeyed. In Hongkong, had the government not imposed severe restrictions on the building of private graves, i.e. graves situated outside authorized cemeteries, the wastage of land would have been equally serious.

The reason for all this trouble about graves lay in the widely held Southern Chinese belief in *fêng shui* (literally, wind and water), or geomancy—the belief that, if the dead are buried in places of favourable geomantic influence, in respect of hills, water, trees, etc., this will be reflected in the wellbeing of the deceased's descendants.

A constant watch had to be kept by the land officers on the illegal construction of private graves. In the case of a wealthy family, such graves were often massive constructions of granite and marble, with golden lettering and steps leading up to the grave platform; and ordering a family to remove an illegal grave was a virtually insuperable task, such being the desperate importance attached to the grave being sited where it was. One simply had to be watchful, and at the mere sight of a man in a rural area carrying cut stone, rush after him and find out what the stone was to be used for.

Shortly after the war, Overflow of Gold came to the office and applied for a forestry permit, covering an extensive area of rising hillside adjacent to his monastery. A forestry permit bestowed the right to plant and own trees, but gave no ownership rights over the land on which the trees were planted.

During the Japanese occupation, nearly every tree in Hongkong which could be used as firewood had been cut down; and the planting of trees—of which, as always, few people understood the importance—was more vital than it had ever been. The Venerable One's visit to the office was, I am told, greeted with little short of acclamation. Here at last—admittedly, he was a Buddhist monk, and it was unlucky to have him around in the office too much, Buddhism being connected with death—but here at last was one man who understood one of the district's major problems, and was seriously prepared to plant trees on a large scale, and look after them.

Which he did. Passing that way by car in my Secretariat days, I remember often glancing up at the otherwise bare hill slopes, and noting with approval that growing forest of Chinese fir. And some months after taking over the district, having dinner one evening with my predecessor, he asked me whether I knew Abbot Kam Moon, on whom he commented:

"He's a funny old chap, but at least one good thing he's done, and that was to plant that forest."

I entirely agreed.

One afternoon the following autumn, I went out to have lunch at the Monastery of the Exalted Eastern Gem.

Of fine Chinese classical construction, built in grey stone with stone-paved courts, with its floating green-tiled roofs and laughing eaves, it was a beautiful reminder of what China is, once past the tenements, the factories, the apartment blocks. Situated in a well-chosen position, it commanded a magnificent view over the distant sea and its islands, one of them (but it took time to recognize it from this unusual angle) being Hongkong itself.

I always enjoyed going there. The Chinese Buddhist vegetarian food was excellent; the monastery grew a specially good hill tea, which was usually served; the monks were most hospitable; and Sik Kam Moon's deputy, who from the spiritual point of view really ran the place, was a Buddhist of some erudition, with whom it was a pleasure to converse. Like many erudite Buddhists, he did not object to liquor; and without word said, a bottle of brandy usually appeared. Overflow of Gold would have been horrified, but he was so occupied with his business affairs that he was never there for lunch.

After lunch, having half an hour to spare before my next appointment, which was in the town far below, I decided to take a stroll through the forest which, most of it now ten years old, stood fine and high, the bushy firs combining, overhead and around, to shield any who entered from the still oppressive warmth of the sun.

I was looking up, admiring the tops of the trees and the broken rays of the sun filtering through them, when I tripped on something, and nearly fell headlong. It was the marble kerb of a large—and new—grave.

My mind whipped round the leading personalities in the nearby town, wondering which of them had recently had a death in the family. Then I looked a little further into the forest.

There was not just one grave. There were not just ten. The graves, all recent, and all belonging to rich Hongkong families (not to local people), were in their fifties. They were—as I discovered, plunging on in silent amazement beneath the trees—in their hundreds. Graves stretched far up the hill, and in all directions. And not one was visible to the public gaze. The trees were old enough to furnish complete concealment.

Due to the degree to which *fêng shui* intruded into the district's problems, it was necessary to understand its principles thoroughly. Now I came to think of it, the hillside, enjoying much the same view as the monastery, had almost perfect *fêng shui*. It pointed to the fact that Abbot Kam Moon, who knew all about *fêng shui* (though as a Buddhist he was supposed not to believe in it), had carefully thought this out ten years or more ago, realizing it was a potential goldmine. The *fêng shui* was so good that the obstacle of the trees, preventing the ancestors from seeing the view as they lay in their graves, did not matter.

Despite everything the Hongkong Government had tried to do to make the authorized city cemeteries attractive, and to ensure they were sited according to the principles of *fêng shui*, no one liked them. The superb *fêng shui* from this lovely country hillside, coupled with Abbot Kam Moon's assurance to each client that they could with impunity evade every government restriction and never be found out, meant that each grave site (situated on land on which the Abbot's only rights concerned the trees) was worth untold thousands of dollars. Out of this single project of his alone, Overflow of Gold had made a fortune.

And he had certainly made good use of his forestry

permit, which cost him, if I remember rightly, about eight dollars a year.

One of the great Buddhist words is the Law. Primarily it means the Sacred Buddhist Law, but it also implies respect for law in general, acknowledging the universality of Buddhism, and its need to conform with the laws of different nations. It is also of note that the Buddhists are one of the very few segments of the Chinese population who are in general litigious. Among the rest, the saying is more often than not, 'Go to the law, go to the devil!'

The fact that so much to do with Buddhism in China has been connected with some scandal or other (of which the case of Kam Moon's forest is, I may say, a most restrained example), when coupled with Buddhist insistence on respect for the law, chastity, celibacy, etc., is one of the main reasons why, to so many millions of Chinese, the word religion, as the West understands it, is a synonym for hypocrisy—another feature of China which is not generally realized in the West. As the old Cantonese saying runs, 'Women who pray to the gods have wicked hearts'.

In the Chinese theatre, a Buddhist monk character is invariably a figure of ridicule and secret fun, while mention of a Buddhist monk produces a laugh as certain as when, in the English theatre, a mother-in-law is mentioned. It is so stock that it is beneath the dignity of a good dramatist to use it.

The discovery of Kam Moon's secret fortune, perfectly hidden beneath desperately needed trees, produced in me a reaction similar to that evoked, on a wider scale, by the British Army officer who, during the Second World War, sold Burma by the grid-square to Indian contractors. It was so absurd—and so perfect—that, though it was wrong, it was impossible to be angry.

It did mean, however, that in the office we kept a closer eye on Abbot Kam Moon's commercial activities, in order to be forearmed, should he try to fool us again.

It happened about this time that among our 'clients' at the office was a young American business man, representing substantial Swiss interests in Basel. He had been authorized by his principals to set up a cotton waste factory but had been having great difficulty in obtaining a site. He was a genial character, widely travelled, and with much charm of manner. I always looked forward to his visits.

A factory for the re-processing of cotton waste—as I think everyone engaged in this occupation will freely admit—is a peculiarly nauseous place. The waste itself, gathered goodness knows where, oily and foul, stinks; and the factory itself—it needs a high chimney—emits an unusually revolting smoke, quite thin to look at, but oily and clinging, and with yet another foul smell. No one, in other words, wants to live or pursue an occupation anywhere near a cotton waste factory.

Our American friend had scoured Kowloon and New Kowloon in his endeavour to find a site. Each time he got on to something remotely suitable there were objections from somebody, usually from the Department of Labour, whose officers, as he explained it, were 'hounding him around', but also from individuals neighbour to the sites. Reluctantly, he had abandoned hope of Kowloon, and come to search in the New Territories, though even with us he was not faring much better.

One of our problems was that our burgeoning industrial zones were situated one on either side of a long-established area of fruit preserving, using traditional Chinese processes, during part of which the fruit is exposed to the open air and sunlight. The greatest care had to be taken over any factory emitting smoke, lest this contaminate the fruit and (as well as possibly poisoning people) damage the reputation of what was, in fact, Hongkong's oldest industry, the most famous of the fruit preservers enjoying the distinction of having been a direct supplier to Queen Victoria. The prospect of eating a preserved plum flavoured with cotton-waste smoke was not enticing.

We tried everything. We studied wind directions and the positions of hills. We discussed smoke-filters and different kinds of chimneys. Occasionally, we thought we had satisfied ourselves; but still, nothing would satisfy the Labour Department. Howard, the American—we were on first-name terms by this time—had spent nearly a month inconclusively examining sites and their possibilities, when one day, coming to my office, he inquired diffidently:

"Could you sell or rent me an island?"

"An entire island?" I asked—it suggested visions of an American warship and a ceremonial hoisting of the Stars and Stripes.

"Well, yes."

"Which one?" I asked guardedly.

He mentioned a name, explaining that he had not yet seen the place, but had heard it might be suitable.

One wall of my office was almost entirely covered by a large-scale map of the district. Studying it together, we found the island concerned.

Situated in what was technically the industrial zone, it was an offshore islet, less than a $\frac{1}{4}$ square mile in size, with about fifty yards of water between it and the mainland. So far as I knew, it was uninhabited.

It had various immediate snags. A piped water-supply would be expensive to install, a jetty would be required, and ferrying *matériel* between islet and mainland would send up costs. But there was no danger of smoke contamination, and (though this I could not divulge) the islet was scheduled in due course to be linked to the mainland by reclamation. I said I thought it sounded a good idea.

"In that case, I'll go and take a look at it," Howard replied.

Two days later I received a call from the Very Venerable Overflow of Gold. He had no previous appointment; but Mr. Lo, saying he thought I would like to see him, ushered him in.

There was a subtlety concealed beneath this. None of the staff were Buddhists, nor did they care twopence about monks. But Westerners, they knew, had a different attitude towards religion. Westerners respected their own Christian priests, for example, and, not wishing to show disrespect to other religions, were inclined to take Buddhist abbots seriously—more seriously than a non-Buddhist Chinese would. Thus, in bringing Overflow of Gold past the detested gate without an appointment, there was a delicate touch of 'You might as well deal with this yourself. You have more time for these people than we have.' A Chinese staff presents an endless series of subtleties of this kind.

Beaming broadly, Sik Kam Moon gave me the Buddhist greeting of clasped palms, and, with a flurry of explanations and apologies, hastened forward to take a seat, on which he—well, I think the nearest word would be splurged. All his curves, the lines of which had been downward on entry, unexpectedly expanded sideways. This always fascinated me. I used to imagine that if I pressed a finger into him, my finger would go in and in, without ever reaching a bone. (Incidentally, his first name, Sik, was the surname adopted by all Chinese Buddhist monks and nuns, being the Buddha's surname, Siddhartha, reduced to a Chinese monosyllable.)

He talked about the monastery; he talked about the trees (but not, of course, about the graves); he wasted quite a lot of time. Then, looking more of an idyll than ever, he imparted to me his latest and most beautiful plan.

It was to be a pleasure garden, with pavilions and a statue of the Buddha, and would be designed as a place of beauty, which the tired people from the city could visit, and where they would find the most perfect repose. It was, he said, something such as no monastery had ever done before; it would be a public service, provided free for the entire population of Hongkong.

Something about this made me suspect, rather uncharitably, that he was about to ask for a subscription. I was wrong, however. It was not a subscription he was after. It was a permit. The pleasure garden would be built on a piece of Crown land—and Sik Kam Moon, on the subject of the status of land, was as accurate as a land officer—to occupy which he would need a permit, which he had come to request.

Hastening on, scarcely taking breath, from the inward mystery of his robes he whisked forth a handful of papers, plans, designs, cheques, accounts. They had all the money required, he showed me; the project would go ahead at once; within two months the pleasure garden would be open to the public. All that was now required was the permit.

"Whereabouts is the land, relative to the monastery?" I asked, trying to get a picture in my mind's eye.

Sik Kam Moon beamed, and shook his head. It was nowhere near the monastery, he explained. The monastery was too high up, too far away. A pleasure garden for the general public had to be nearer things; and a perfect site had been chosen, something quite unique. It was a beautiful little island situated just off the shore.

"Which island?" I inquired a trifle sourly.

He named it caressingly.

It was the islet Howard was interested in.

"Now, look here," I said, "I don't want to be discouraging. I think your idea for a public garden is charming. But that, I'm afraid, is not the right place for it. The whole of that area is scheduled for industrialization, and in a year or two will be a mass of factories—not the kind of place people will get much pleasure visiting."

Not in the least put off, he pursued his argument for a garden. Adjacent factories would not matter in the least, the garden would be so beautiful.

It proved impossible to convince him otherwise; and in the end, after much argument, I was obliged to refuse flatly to discuss the matter any more. He departed shakily, looking worried and upset.

The same afternoon, Howard telephoned. He was interested in the islet, he said, but would need a few days in which to work out a revised set of costings, after which he would have to consult his principals in Basel. He would let me know something in about ten days.

During this time, Kam Moon visited the office every day, importuning one clerk after another, begging them to make me change my mind, until everyone was bored stiff with him. These attempts having failed, on the seventh day he submitted a formal written application to purchase the islet by public auction in building-and-garden status.

The application would have to be thrown out, of course, the land being reserved for industry. But this was not what was worrying me.

One way and another, Howard had had a great deal of opposition to contend with. Had he been a Chinese, I would have been unconcerned about this, feeling confident that he would know how to deal with such matters. But, in the case of an American, unfamiliar with the district, there was the suggestion—and Kam Moon's evident determination to block Howard seemed particularly to bear it out—that he had unintentionally been treading on people's toes.

In the city, this would not have mattered. But this was the country; and when establishing oneself in the country it is always desirable to advance along carefully laid lines of local goodwill, or things will go wrong. It would be useless Howard trying to set up a factory on that islet, if local opinion was for some reason against it—which was what it looked like.

"I don't want to worry you," I said to him, next time he called, "but are you aware of any local opposition there might be to your occupying that islet?"

"Opposition?" he exclaimed. "Not that I know of. It was the local people who put me on to it."

He named two leading merchants in a nearby town. They were not Buddhists, and might thus well be opposed to anything Kam Moon was doing. It suggested that Howard might have landed himself on the wrong side of some local power struggle.

"Who's opposing it?" he asked me.

"I'm afraid I can't tell you. It's rather a curious kind of opposition. I don't understand it myself. You wouldn't be conscious of having offended someone locally?"

"Surely not! " he said emphatically.

"Did anyone see you visit the island?"

"No—only the man who ferried us across."

"Who was he?"

"No one special. IIe just happened to be there with a sampan."

"Does anyone live on the island?"

"No."

"You're sure?"

"Absolutely sure. The only inhabitants are those goddam African snails," he commented with a grin.

I groaned. It was the height of the snail season, and not a flower in my garden had come up.

"All right," I concluded. "Don't worry about it. I'll make some inquiries and see if we can't settle it."

After he left, I sent for the land officer, a young Eurasian, who was in charge of the area.

"Kam Moon, in my opinion, is up to something on that island. You don't think it's another grave site, do you?"

He laughed.

"There are no trees on it! "

"No," I said. "Not yet. But we don't want to walk into another of his traps. What I think we must do is inspect the island, but at some rather unlikely hour. Could you meet me tomorrow at seven in the morning and drive me out to have a quick look?"

We did this. It was a fine, hot summer morning, and the roads being clear at that hour we made it in about thirty minutes. Leaving the car, we mounted a grassy slope to gain a better view of the surroundings.

Though close to a town, the place was unexpectedly lonely. There were no habitations, and no one was about. Before us lay the islet, a tumpy hillock of rock and rough grass. As Howard had said, no one seemed to live on it. No fishing boats were near it. On our side of the shore an unattended sampan was beached. Apart from this there was no sign of life. There was no visible clue to what we were after.

"Well, one thing I'm sure," I said resignedly, as we started back down the slope; "he doesn't want it as a pleasure garden. But—"

And, at that moment, we both stopped. It was a windless morning, and on the gravel track, coming from inland, could be heard the crunch of approaching footsteps.

We waited, feeling strangely like conspirators, as along the track below us came the Venerable Abbot. Before him he was carrying a piece of old, stained cloth, using it as a sack, and which was full of something. Following him were a young grey-smocked novice, and a villager, each with a pole over his shoulder, from which dangled two large wicker baskets such as are used in China for carrying live ducks. The interstices of the wicker had been filled up with brown paper, and it was impossible to see what they contained.

The Abbot must have realized we were there, because of the car, but he made no sign of having seen us. The little procession passed along to the sampan, in which the duck baskets were carefully placed. The Abbot then embarked with his sack, and a minute or so later, the villager was ferrying the three of them across to the islet.

There they disembarked, and the Abbot, going some way up into the rough grass, gently laid his sack on the ground, and with little movements tipped the contents out. Then the duck baskets were opened, and their contents were similarly tipped out, with loving care.

We were too far away to see what they were exactly, but Howard had already provided the clue.

They were giant African snails—live ones. Since very early morning (the best time for catching them) the Abbot had been going round the grassy precincts of his monastery (but not, of course, in any farmer's field) picking them up, hundreds of them, to bring to this islet, as an act of merit—to preserve life.

The islet was the only possible sanctuary in the neighbourhood for the pestilential animals, and now this final sanctuary was threatened. Abbot Kam Moon's proposed pleasure garden was his last-ditch stand in defence of the snails.

Furthermore, the fate from which he rescued them (of being killed by farmers) differed little from the fate to which he consigned them. On the islet there was no cultivated vegetation suitable for the snails to eat; and the giant African snail is, among other things, a cannibal.

By the Abbot's act of merit, the snails were left to devour one another in silence.

My land officer had said nothing. I took a cautious glance at him. He was shaking from head to foot with laughter. So, after an instant, was I. What other possible reaction was there? The reaction, in sum, of a Chinese theatre audience at the merest mention of a monk.

Struggling to prevent ourselves from laughing aloud, we raced down the hill, leapt into the car and, once out of earshot, howled with laughter all the way back to Kowloon. So did the entire office when we told them. I have seldom seen such a commotion.

"Gee, it's unreal," Howard muttered, when I explained it to him. "But I haven't the heart to interfere with the old boy. Guess I'd better find another site."

II

A Malevolent Dragon

DURING THE KOREAN WAR, boom conditions prevailed in Hongkong, and concurrently, deposits of wolfram were discovered on one of the district's larger islands. Wolfram, used in the making of munitions, was in sudden international demand, and the price of it had risen.

The deposits were found in a rugged, uninhabited area entirely devoid of communications, about 1,200 feet above sea level, miles from any population centre. Report of the discovery spread throughout urban Hongkong like wildfire, causing one of those stampede movements which one comes to expect in a Chinese population, whenever something exciting happens. Thousands of people who had never before heard of the island, and had no idea where it was, set out for it and reached the wolfram deposits within a matter of hours—itself no mean feat.

A mining company had taken out a licence for the area, but its representatives were powerless to protect their rights in the face of such an invasion of humanity. An entire police force would have been required to safeguard the company's position. With probably a good deal of the rough stuff which traditionally goes with mining, the company was obliged to treat the invaders as sub-licensees, in most cases purchasing mined wolfram from them. Permitted or not permitted—and allowing for fights and upheavals, the situation changed every week—hundreds of men and women set to, with such implements as they possessed, and all but flung themselves into the steep green hillsides.

There were no building materials available, and to have brought such materials to so inaccessible a spot would have been uneconomical, since everything would have had to be carried up a soaringly steep mountainside on people's backs, after a two-hour walk through a ricefield area, and a four-hour journey by boat from Hongkong.

The outcome was that the miners, like rabbits, lived almost entirely inside the hill, the only outer sign of their existence being the spoil cast out from the holes that gave access to their warren. As the weeks passed, the extent of their burrowings enlarged, the warren developing into a complete underground—or in-hill—town. A digging made unsuccessfully for a few yards in one direction would be abandoned and become a cavern house or shop. Where a disused digging was fairly high, two- and three-storey apartments came into being. Eventually there were streets, street-lighting, crossroads, market-places, and residential *quartiers*, all inside the hill; and, Chinese being civilized people, these were well-organized, sprinkled with cafés, bars and brothels.

The district administration's official attitude was that the place was an absolute disgrace; but as my predecessor confessed to me privately, it was difficult not to find it all rather endearing. And no one could deny it was unusual.

By the time I came to the district, the Korean War had ended, the price of wolfram had fallen and, except for five or six of the more persistent, the mining community had melted away into the city. The miners' town was silent and empty, as gloomy as a Roman catacomb. The sole significant survivor on the hillside, carrying on in its own buildings as if nothing remarkable had occurred, was the mining company. This was controlled by European interests, the site manager being a Dutchman.

With the government's agreement, the company had extended its area under licence; but when mining operations started in this new area, adjacent to the first and equally high, violent objections were lodged at our office by two villages situated in the coastal, rice-growing valleys 1,200 feet below the mine. The villagers claimed that the rib of mountainside, into which the miners were cutting—a steeply descending rib, running down almost to the sea, and which separated the two villages, which were in different valleys—was, according to the principles of *fêng shui*, the spine of a dragon; and that to cut into it would hurt and anger the dragon, causing it to become malevolent. This would be a threat to the villages, involving pestilence, the death of eldest sons, and similar tragedies.

The *heung cheung* of the larger of the two villages came to see me, and informed me that, since the day the miners first touched the dragon's spine, one boy had died in the village and six others had been seriously ill. To me, judging by the size of the village, and by the season of the year, which was spring, these figures did not sound in the least abnormal. The incidence of children's diseases is highest in spring, and such diseases are often serious, frequently infectious and occasionally fatal—but I could not say so. The *heung cheung* seemed genuinely, and with anxiety, to attribute it to the wrath of the dragon.

I checked with the Chinese medical officer in charge of the district hospital, from which regular medical patrols visited all these villages. He confirmed the *heung cheung's* figures; and he also confirmed my view that they were not abnormal.

Did the *heung cheung* really believe the dragon had become malevolent? Or was it that, partly believing it, and knowing that government in the New Territories (where there was no Revolution of 1912) was more old-fashioned than in China, he considered he might use it as a convenient weapon of argument? Or was it that he did not believe it at all, but knew that Europeans thought Chinese *did* believe in such things, so that consequently, when a Chinese *heung cheung* spoke of *fêng shui*, it meant that a European official had to sit up and take notice?

These three questions recurred in my mind every time I had to handle a matter connected with village *fêng shui*, and I do not think I ever gave myself an answer which I could have sworn was correct. The *fêng shui* of graves is an altogether simpler subject. With an understanding of the general principles of Chinese geomancy, one simply has to stand at the grave site, orientate one's body correctly, and one can see at a glance whether or not the place has good *fêng shui*.

In villages, with their dragons and old lore, it is more complex. *Fêng shui* was a universal concept in the district. Every rib of every hill, every spur, every eminence, from end to end of the district, was the abode of some sleeping dragon or tiger—*was* a dragon or a tiger, in fact—and it would have been beyond the capacity of the most learned *fêng shui* expert to have identified them all.

For example, when finally I visited the villages situated below the wolfram mine, I could have sworn that the dragon's spine was the rib of mountain inside which the mining rush had taken place. The dragon, in my opinion, had already had several vertebrae removed, and had not minded in the least.

Not so, I was informed. That was not the dragon's spine.

Climb up to the top of the real spine, and I would understand.

So I climbed to the top. It is one of the steepest slopes in South China, and it was one of the hottest days of the year. At the top, when I had removed from round my eyes the perspiration which was blinding me, I looked down and around me, and I still could not understand what the villagers meant. To my eyes, the already-mined rib was the dragon's spine.

But the villagers were consistent, and very specific. The mining company had bored into the spine—the villagers' one—at a point which I felt sure would have done the dragon an injury. But no. That part of the mining operation did not matter. It was fifty feet higher up, where a second bore had been started, which was the dangerous place, I was informed.

The two points of bore entry, in my view, differed in nothing. I found it incomprehensible. But every time during the next two years, when the company unobtrusively tried to start again on the higher of the two points, there was an outcry, police had to be rushed to the scene to prevent violence, while in Kowloon I had to drop whatever I was doing, and journey out to the place—it took a day and a night to get there and back—in order to talk to the people and restore calm.

The villagers, it will be concluded, believed passionately in *fêng shui*.

Yes, up to a point they did. But in cases of village *fêng shui*, this is never the whole story. When *fêng shui* is brandished as a weapon, beside this—*beside* it, not concealed behind it—lies another reason for the protest, usually a material reason. On the village side, it is indelicate to refer to this, and on the official side, it is bad manners to ask questions about it. If, as an official, one feels it essential to know exactly what this material reason is, one is reduced to finding out by deduction. But usually this is not necessary. The mere knowledge that there always *is* a material reason, in addition to the psychic reason concerned with geomancy, is often sufficient to lead one to it inadvertently.

In this particular instance, the mining company had omitted to do something which the villagers desired, in the sense that by this omission the company was behaving improperly. They should perhaps have given a tea party to the two villages, or made a present to the *heung cheung*, or an offering at the village temple, or perhaps they should have given the villagers some cement to repair a watercourse or a path. It could have been one of many things, depending on the tradition of the village; and by living in the village for a few days one could easily have found out. The company personnel, Europeans and Westernized Chinese, had been living comparatively near the village but had made no attempt to find out. They had thus given offence.

So, the Western mind will reason, the villagers did not really believe in their dragon at all. They were merely using the dragon as a blind, in order to squeeze some money out of the mining company.

Nothing could be further from the truth. They did, up to a point, believe in their dragon. *Fêng shui* is fundamental in Chinese ideas.

But, just as Chinese approach religious ideas with what I have called earlier a negative eclecticism, so is it in respect of their belief in geomancy, and in much else. The fact is, to say that the villagers *believed* in geomancy is to use too strong a word, while to say they *posited* it would be to use

too weak a word. Chinese approach to their own fundamental ideas lies in what, in the Western mind, is an empty
space situated halfway between a belief and a posit.

Viewing things thus, the villagers saw nothing questionable about brandishing their dragon with one hand, while
expecting to have some money put into the other. There
was no concealment about it, either—nor, as mentioned
earlier, may it even have been actual cash they were after.
It was simply that it was not good manners to talk about it.

The village youth, when out of hearing of their elders,
would confess with a laugh that they did not believe in
fêng shui, giving the unwary Westerner the impression that
the Chinese mind was changing. But I have seen many
such youths grow up, and have often been startled to hear
them, at the age of thirty or so, giving a long and involved
explanation of something which does not make sense
until—with a mental jerk—one clocks on to the fact that
what one has been listening to is a modern rationalization
of *fêng shui*.

Such a young man from the countryside, considering
himself more modern-minded than his elders, seldom cares
to admit that he believes/posits such ideas. Among city-
dwellers and the well educated, there is far less reticence,
particularly in the matter of graves. This of course does not
imply that such people believe in actual dragons, any more
than the Lord Mayor of London does, though he has a
dragon over his door. The dragon and the tiger, in Chinese
geomancy, are figurative expressions; but they embody ideas
that are profoundly impressed upon the Chinese mind.

The siting of graves shows geomancy at its clearest, since
in this matter it is geomancy undiluted by other considera-
tions. Highly educated Chinese, if they do not know you
very well, will sometimes tell you they themselves do not

believe in geomancy. If this happens, all I can say is, order the removal of their ancestor's grave and see what happens.

In introducing *fêng shui* in the preceding chapter, I described it as a Southern Chinese belief. Actually, under various names, geomantic concepts are more or less universal in China, though their importance varies from province to province. Geomancy is pre-eminently connected with hills, valleys and water, and is thus prominent in the South, which is hilly and often mountainous. But even in the flatter provinces, geomantic concepts are widely in evidence, even in people's homes—in the arrangement of furniture in rooms, and in the positioning of doors and windows.

Nowhere is geomancy more prominent than in Kwangtung; and looking at the map of China, and observing how far away Kwangtung is from the Chinese capital, this at first suggests that geomancy may be no more than an archaism of a distant and backward province.

In this respect, the map of China is deceptive. Kwangtung, though far from the capital, is one of the 'heart' provinces of China—Hunan and Szechuan are among the other 'heart' provinces—from which often come the influences which determine the way for the people as a whole. Kwangtung is also the most conservative of the provinces, and proud of being so, guarding old customs and traditions in their original forms, when these in other parts of China have been allowed to change.

The Cantonese language is a striking example of this conservatism. A poem of the fifth century A.D. no longer rhymes in modern standard Chinese; but read the same poem in Cantonese and it rhymes instantly. Cantonese almost certainly has a close kinship to standard Chinese as it was spoken 1,500 years ago. As with so much else in

Kwangtung, it has been handed down sticking closely to its original form.

As the Hunanese regard their province as the sword-bearing conscience of China, so do the Cantonese regard themselves as the guardians of tradition, the guardians of China's soul. Kwangtung is not an Outer Province, though Chinese prime ministers sometimes wish it were.

There is a tendency in the West to regard as invalid assumptions about China made on the basis of Cantonese experience, and in particular of experience in Hongkong. This is, I believe, unjust. Naturally, each province of China presents a different aspect of that enormous country; but a description of the people in any one province will reveal many things common to all; and Kwangtung representing an extreme in China, which it does in numerous ways, is as good a sounding-board as any. Kwangtung represents much that is oldest and most obdurate in China. Hit your head against the wall of Kwangtung and it will hurt you more than in any other province. When it comes to explaining a country to one who has not been there, this is, I believe, an advantage. The tones in the picture are extreme—precisely as they should be in a good press photograph. As a Chinese friend of mine, who is from another province, once observed to me, "Kwangtung is like a dictionary. You refer to it when you need accurate information."

As to Hongkong, the advantage of experience there is that Cantonese there behave naturally, without political inhibitions; while as to the New Territories, they are of course unique, a living museum piece, a delightful relic of the Ch'ing dynasty which, avoiding any direct experience of the Revolutions of 1912 and 1949, has come almost unscathed into the world of television and transistor radios. Nor, as these pages perhaps show, can the area be labelled

175

'unrepresentative, influenced by the British'. Rather the contrary. The moment the Special Magistrate tried to do anything British, everything went wildly wrong; and in the end it was useless to deny that he had been far more influenced by the New Territories than they by him.

As a key to understanding modern China, the district provided few clues. But as a means to drawing a little nearer to China's soul—which was and will be—it often seemed to me to serve as a strangely revealing byway.

My last visit to the wolfram mine is one of my after-dinner stories, though at the time it was not in that light that I saw it.

The dispute between the villages and the mining company continued, with various alarums and excursions. Then, in my third spring in the district, a deputation from the larger village came to my office and complained bitterly that the company had broken its agreement with them to share the existing water supply, completely depriving the village of its main source of water for the ricefields.

This source was a substantial stream which flowed down, almost as steeply as a waterfall, from a strong mountain spring situated 1,600 feet above the village. Four hundred feet below the spring, the company, by agreement with the village, tapped half the water for their own use, leaving the rest to descend normally. Since the past few days, the deputation informed me, the company had been taking all the water. At the village level the stream-bed was dry. The rice was already green in the fields; and if water was not flooded on the fields within the next few days, the entire crop would be ruined.

I wrote at once to the mining company, which had an office in town. In reply came a letter saying that the company had made no alteration to its water arrangements, and more or less adding that the villagers were talking non-sense. A few days after this came another letter, saying that the site manager had been in town; the water arrangements had been thoroughly inspected and the villagers' complaint was entirely without foundation.

Meanwhile, every day someone came from the village to implore us to take action before it was too late and they lost their rice crop.

The situation was that the company was sick to death with us, believing that our motto was 'Villager, right or wrong', while on our side we were sick to death of the whole thing, including the villagers.

"Are you sure the company has tampered with the supply?" I asked. "They assure me they haven't."

The village emissaries were sure.

"Has anyone climbed up there to have a look?"

No, this was not necessary. They *knew*.

"How can you know unless you've been up? How d'you know the spring hasn't run dry?"

They were sure it hadn't.

"Has anyone been up to take a look at it?"

No. This too was not necessary. The spring never dried up.

"But how d'you know that this year it *hasn't*?"

They knew.

They *knew*! China's spoiled children! Never walk up a hill, of course! It meant once more that *I* had to climb up and find out *for* them.

It meant my going because, as we had learned by experience, the Europeans in the company looked down on Chinese, even on their own employees, treating them as inferiors. This meant that I could not send Ah Kuen or Mr. Lo, because the European manager would give them no respect; and my one European land officer had by this time retired.

"What a perfect nuisance Europeans are in this district!" I exclaimed aloud exasperatedly.

Exactly, be it noted, what a Chinese official would have said. We see ourselves more clearly when we sit in the opposite seat.

The spring was verging into summer, and it was already very warm. I baulked at climbing that infernal hill, which in some places reached the extreme point beyond which a walk becomes a climb. Instead, I resolved to go by a more lenient route, though to a higher altitude: to a mountain-dominated plateau situated 1,600 feet above sea level, where I could stay the night at a Buddhist monastery, examine the spring, then descend to the mine, then descend to the village—altogether less exhausting than doing it the other way.

Combining various jobs, as we always had to when travelling, we got through surprisingly early, reaching the monastery for lunch instead of (as I had anticipated) for dinner. After a pleasant vegetarian meal—my cook, knowing where I was going, had providentially stuffed a flask in among my night kit—we made our way (I had with me Ah Kuen and a demarcator) through a wild area of rough grass, the almost wall-like slopes of the mountain descending only a few yards away from us. After some time, moisture and brown grass-roots beneath our feet warned us we were nearing the spring.

Well, there was no doubt the villagers 1,600 feet below were right about the spring. It was bubbling up so strongly that the little waves it created were making a swishing sound against the grass; and as we followed the stream to the edge of the sharply descending slope of the mountain, it could be seen that, even divided by two, it should have been giving the village an excellent supply.

I had hoped to be able to see, from this high spot, if there was anything the matter, and, if so, what it was. But the descent was almost sheer; the take-off point, 400 feet below, was in shadow; and nothing could be seen. It meant crawling down in the grass to the mine level, examining the take-off, returning to the mine and probably negotiating, then crawling up again to the plateau—a painful business in the heat, but we had already ensconced ourselves at the monastery in preparation for the night, and there was certainly nowhere else to sleep.

The European mine manager would probably have put me up; but he would, I knew, do nothing for Ah Kuen and the demarcator. This would separate me from them, and lead them to suppose, should the situation with the villagers deteriorate, that the manager and I had come to a private agreement. At all costs the three of us had to stick together.

I looked at my watch. It was 2 p.m. With luck I could reach the plateau again before sundown.

"You two stay up here and wait for me," I said. "It won't take long."

Leaving them seated contentedly, their legs dangling over the grassy edge of the slope, I half-scrambled, half-crawled down into the green-blue shadow.

Reaching the mine level, which was on a spur, from which the dragon's spine descended, I re-entered the sunlight. There was no one about. Finding, after some search, a fast-flowing watercourse, truly racing along a well-built brick runnel, I set off in the direction whence the water came, re-entered the shadow and soon found myself edging round a precipice of damp rock, walking step by step along the brick watercourse, which was all that separated me from a tumble into an anonymity of rock and bushy growth, amid which it was unlikely that any search party would have found me.

I had counted on reaching the stream in about ten minutes. It actually took more like forty minutes, due to the distance, the undergrowth, and to various obstacles. The shadow and the damp made it no cooler. My legs were soon trembling with the strain of balancing. My hands were cut and filthy, from having to support myself occasionally against the rock. And I was very angry.

But, when eventually I reached the stream, such was the simplicity of the problem that my anger dissipated. There came the water, tumbling down from high above—at this point, actually a waterfall for a foot or so. But there was no mechanical device to ensure a division of what went to the mine, and what continued to fall to the village far below. Practical and entirely in keeping with the surroundings, they had used the old country method, conveying water to the runnel by means of a piece of thick bamboo, spliced and wired into position, so that half the contents of the waterfall should normally have fallen into it. A small stone, falling from somewhere above, had landed in the runnel, hitting the bamboo and causing it to tilt upward slightly at the other end, whereupon the wires, not very well adjusted, had swung the bamboo out, so that the whole of the waterfall was now falling into it. Scarcely a drop was going down the hill.

No one from the mining company had troubled to inspect it; no villager had come up to look at it. Had they done so, the thing could have been solved by a single movement of the hand. Rather than put themselves to this trouble, they had protested on the one side and struck attitudes on the other, leaving it to the dogsbody administration to find out what the trouble was. This, it seemed, was what administrators were paid for.

I decided not to touch it. The mining people had to see this for themselves, to prevent recurrences. Laboriously I struggled back along the difficult track.

As I at last emerged into the sunlight on the mining spur, the Dutch manager was coming out of his asbestos bungalow-cum-office. He was short and tough, aged about forty, with short-cut golden hair, blue eyes, a ruddy, lined face, and a square mouth.

I introduced myself.

"You've come up about this water, I suppose," the Dutchman said caustically—he spoke excellent English.

"Yes."

"The village people have nothing to complain of. We have already inspected their complaint."

"So have I," I said. "I have just come back from doing so. And the villagers have everything to complain of. You are depriving them of their entire water and ruining their crops."

I explained what had gone wrong with the bamboo. He listened in silence, then said coolly:

"I don't believe you. Your office listens to what the village people say, never to what we say."

"I'm not prepared to argue about that," I replied. "The villagers, I admit, are troublesome, but on this point they have reason to be. Without realizing it, you are breaking your agreement with them. Now, will you please send someone to the water source, and re-adjust the bamboo. It's a very simple job once you get there."

Without trace of emotion, he looked round the bare mountainside.

"Where is there someone to send?" he asked superciliously. "My men are all busy."

They were evidently all underground somewhere. I was becoming desperate.

"Then will you yourself come with me, and have a look at it. I'm prepared to go a second time, if you will. But somebody must see this thing as a matter of urgency, and put it right."

He looked at me for a moment expressionlessly:

"I too am busy," he replied.

He was unbudgable.

"Listen to me," I said firmly. "Are you going to re-adjust that bamboo, or are you not?"

"It is not necessary," he answered coldly.

It was a glorious blue afternoon, edging to evening. In the distance the blue and mauve mountains of China stretched to the far horizon. Below, on the placid sea, a white steamer with a wake behind it was making its way to Macao.

We were two men on a mountain. I had, to some extent, authority over that mountain, and over everyone on it. But where does authority lie when there are just two of you? In two fists?

I was walking with a Malacca cane, with which I could have dealt him a pretty ugly blow. What good would it have done? In sixty seconds he would have reduced me to unconscious pulp, which would be a nuisance; I would probably lose a tooth and be late for dinner at the monastery.

Out of the corner of my eye, I saw my two men, far up on the ridge; I suppose they thought the two of us were discussing the current movies.

What does one do in such a situation? I was the government, and the government is power. But what is power, when it comes to it? Power, in the final resort, is opinion. It is opinion which provides the force that facilitates action. There was no opinion on that mountain, neither behind me, nor behind him.

There was nothing else for it. I took a deep breath, and as if listening to someone else's voice, said:

"I command you, in the Queen's name, to inspect the source of your water supply, or send some responsible person to do so, forthwith!"

There was a long silence. Far below, the steamer pursued its interminable course. I never felt such a fool in my life.

Was he going to hit me? I could feel him wondering whether he would. Assessing him more keenly, his expression suggested incredulity. Finally, his lips curled slightly, and he said:

"I'll send my Chinese assistant."

Knowing his attitude towards Chinese people, I realized this was meant to be insulting, but I swallowed it. I knew the assistant by repute. He was a graduate from an American university, a young man of thoroughness, who would do the job properly.

With deliberate slowness, the Dutchman walked towards his bungalow.

"You'd better tell your assistant to hurry," I said. "In an hour it'll be dark, and it's a difficult place to get to."

He did not alter his pace.

After an interminable wait, he re-emerged with his assistant. Once satisfied that the latter was on his way, I bid the Dutchman good-day, and started crawling and scrambling up the slope to rejoin my men.

Below me I could see the Dutchman, an object diminishing in distance. He had not moved. Staring after me, I imagine he may have been wondering what kind of government this was, that was content for its magistrates to crawl over the hills like monkeys.

That night, around 9 p.m., as we later learned, the village had water, and the rice was saved.

The Dutchman subsequently lodged a formal complaint against me to the government, alleging that I had thrown my weight about, using insulting language; and doubtless, wherever he is today, he is repeating the same story, showing how badly British officials behave.

God save the Queen!

12

Three Cows and Two Women

THE DUTCHMAN'S COMPLAINT, though groundless, none the less raises a point on which I feel I owe the reader an explanation. This concerns the rough-and-ready way in which the Special Magistrate can be seen to have handled some of the cases in his court. Dealing with that improbable wall through the squatter shops, for example, he was seen not to hesitate to insult a man across his desk, and on various other occasions he will have been found addressing people accusingly, in a manner which in most countries would be considered highly improper.

Lest this should convey the impression that Hongkong's rural population were treated—at least verbally—with some of the brutal methods of autocracy, and that my earlier explanation of the unique relations between government and people in the New Territories is belied by what I have myself shown of the way in which I handled cases, it should be explained that my outspoken utterances when dealing with people were part of a technique, rendered necessary by the extreme reluctance of country people—and of many townspeople as well—to bring forward facts. As will have been observed from the outset, people had a tendency to sit in court mum, leaving it to you to find out what a case was about. Yet, at the end of it all, as in the office we knew all too well, they would complain if they considered they had not been given a fair hearing.

I think it is probably true to say that every district officer who has ever served in the New Territories has been conscious of this difficulty, and that most of them have found it necessary to evolve a technique, personal to themselves, with which to deal with it.

My own technique, when faced with people who would not come out with facts, was to annoy them, even with abuse where necessary, until, aroused and coming to their own self-defence, they would sometimes involuntarily trick out some preciously needed fact. It was an imperfect technique, but it was the one—I should say with shame—which came most naturally to me; and the fact that the clerk-interpreters took to it so readily, suggested that I was not the first and only person to have used it.

The same was again suggested by the fearlessness with which everyone, high and low, faced such verbal assaults, and by the fact that the office was usually filled to overflowing with people and problems, problems and people, many of whom knew us personally, and who would therefore not have approached us had they been doubtful of our methods, or disapproved of them.

The truth surely is: in a village court, why not speak in a village way? People will understand you better. And the frequency with which a sharp word from the magistrate met with a sharp answer from a villager demonstrated that, when people would consent to speak, they could do so with no holds barred.

As a European, of course, I found many aspects of the Chinese life that came before us in the court more irritating than did my Chinese staff, by whom such things were regarded as normal. As has already been noted, the Special Magistrate and the balloon did not always rise together. There were moments—quite a few of them—in which, seen in retrospect, the *ex*-magistrate would wish to have acted other than he did. But all of these concerned the *conduct* of cases (during which the magistrate released some fury over something or other), none of them their outcome.

Still—and here both the Special Magistrate and the *ex*-magistrate will disclose what has till now been a secret—it always warmed the cockles of my heart when a member of the staff lost his temper with a member of the public. It showed that I was not the only one.

Best of all was it when the entire staff lost their temper—at once, as it were. Only one case, in my experience, provoked this satisfying situation. But it was a case which returned to us several times; and as, on each successive return, the tempers of the staff rose somewhat higher, so did it become progressively more heart-warming.

I had a love-hate relationship towards it. *Qua* case, it was infuriating. But, listening to the effect it produced on the office staff, I found it irresistible. It was never necessary to be told when the case had returned. Far down at the other end of the building, pandemonium in the general office indicated that it had—pandemonium amid which, I must confess again with shame, I listened for the singularly reassuring sound of each member of my staff, one by one, barking in fury at the disputants.

The disturbance—it occurred seven times over a period of three months—was caused by two women, related to each other, living in two obscure hill villages in the eastern part of the district.

From such a beautiful part of the country—green, hilly and entirely unspoilt—one would have expected nothing but idylls. The two women, on the contrary, displayed a degree of fury with each other such as I have seldom seen.

187

They arrived apparently in the same bus, quietly it was said. They sat quietly in the office until their case was called. And then it began.

It resembled a virtuoso operatic performance staged specially for our benefit. *Fortissimo* from the start, they would abuse each other, shouting at the tops of their voices, their sarcasms accompanied by dramatic shoulder-poses and contemptuous tiltings-down of the eyelids. Most of the time they shrieked at each other simultaneously. The noise was terrific. Occasionally someone else managed to get a word in, but these were mere *recitative* passages, their intervals marked by snorts of fury and sniffs of disdain, quickly to be followed by another full-blast aria.

They were in dispute over three cows, in the ownership of which each woman claimed a half-share; and as the two women lived in different villages, it can be seen there was a problem. How the office staff dealt with it I do not know. I am not sure that anyone got as far as that. On the first occasion when the women were brought in to me, however, it seemed that the first step was to obtain a valuation of the cows.

This brought in a fresh complication. One of the cows was a calf. Since none of us could persuade the two women to agree to anything, it meant sending them home each time to think over what we had said, after which, a week or so later, they would come again and stage a fresh performance.

Meanwhile, as the weeks went by, the calf was growing up, and increasing in value. Each session thus had to be commenced by someone making a revised valuation, during which the women—both of them together—reached their highest pitch of anger and emotion, not with each other, but with us. It was usually at this point that whoever happened to be dealing with the women lost his temper with them, and shouted back.

During the three months we had the dispute on our hands, I reckon nearly all of us shouted at them, but they never took the point. When we started, it only made things worse. But I truly believe none of us could help it. There was something about the way the women carried on. They were irritating to a degree provoking me sometimes to wonder whether a main reason why they came was because to see us aroused gave them satisfaction.

But the case gave me satisfaction, too.

Shortly after they had been to see us for the sixth time—refusing, as usual, to agree to any of our suggestions—I unexpectedly chanced upon a possible new line in dealing with them. The next time pandemonium in the general office indicated that they had arrived, I should really have sent for them at once.

But I didn't. The staff, in their own quiet way, had played numerous little games with me. It was now my turn, in my own quiet way, to play a little game with them. I could not resist sitting there, quietly listening, as the tumult drew nearer and became more vociferous.

The case mounted, as it were, in the direction of the more exalted offices; and one by one, each office was in turn reduced to exasperation by the two women. Daily-familiar voices were heard reaching unexpectedly high registers. Normally reserved and sober citizens, fathers of families and models of propriety, could be heard yelling hell and damnation. When the case reached the land officers—it was sent to them in order to keep it away from me—the noise was tremendous. The European senior land officer (he was still with us at that date) was an ex-sergeant-major, and after roaring like a lion at the women, he expelled them bodily into the passage.

It was marvellous.

At last, stiff with rage, snorting and undaunted—they were afraid of no one—the women were brought in to me. On a former occasion, I had been obliged to tell them that unless they kept quiet, I would order that the calf be cut in two, and divided equally between them; and of all the people in the office, they loved me least.

There they stood, sullen and seething. Aware that my outbursts were apt to be more stentorian even than the sergeant-major's (dramatic training tells), they were braced for it, ready on their part to deliver a bravura display of outraged arpeggii.

But I was having a pleasant afternoon. I quietly drummed my fingers on the desk.

"Mr. Lo, ask them if they've any relatives in America, would you?"

He looked at me doubtfully.

"Yes," I continued. "I happened to pass through their villages the other day, and found that nearly every adult man from there lives in New York."

Mr. Lo gave a surprised laugh, and asked the women a question. There was a moment of dumbfounded silence, followed by a curt answer.

Indeed they had a relative in New York. He was the husband of one, brother of the other.

"When was he last here?" I inquired.

He had been away eleven years.

"Kindly give his name and address to Mr. Lo before you leave," I said. "That's all for today, thank you."

Baffled for once, they glared at me in silence, and after a little trouble were persuaded to leave the room. There was a renewal of heart-warming pandemonium in the general office, with clerks shouting at the tops of their voices, before the women finally departed. This was only to be expected, of course. They had been thwarted of their grand finale with me.

A New York address written in Chinese needs a little disentangling, but we finally worked it out. It was a rather superior Chinese restaurant in the East Forties. Summoning the stenographer, I dictated a letter. It read as follows:

Sir,

For several months past we have been importuned by two women members of your family, desiring that we should give attention to a matter which seems to us to involve the equitable division between them of three cows.

We do not contest your right to sail away to America, and remain there for eleven years without seeing your family. We would simply draw it to your notice that we do not consider it among our duties to be required to solve irreconcilable mathematical problems.

If, as we presume, you persist in your present way of living, will you kindly, and forthwith, so arrange your domestic affairs that your womenfolk peaceably enjoy possession of their cows, in such manner as you may see fit, and henceforth cease disturbing us.

We are, etc.

In English it was a fairly pointed letter. In its final Chinese version it was thunderous. As I affixed my red Chinese seal to it, I felt like an emperor.

It worked, too. We never heard from them again.

13

Cables: Solomon

THE DAY CAME WHEN the Special Magistrate—he will
not be squeamish about it—outrivalled Solomon in his
wisdom.

By accident, of course.

It so happened that, situated almost opposite our office,
on the other side of Nathan Road, was Hongkong's most
famous noodle-shop. They were accommodating people
there, and for no extra charge—but for a tip at Chinese
New Year—a young boy would bring over to the office a
complete noodle lunch, steaming hot, the dish sealed by a
metal cover, set on a tray which held, in addition, a small
bowl of soya sauce, another small bowl of mustard and red
pepper sauce, and chopsticks wrapped in a paper napkin.
The noodles being second to none, on hard-pressed days,
when there was no time to go out for lunch, quite a number of us availed ourselves of this agreeable service.

Midday had passed and I was listening to a case concerning a husband with two furiously quarrelling wives.
They were from a rural part of the district. The husband
was seated before me, his wives on either side of him.
With them had come the village elder, who had insisted
that the case be brought to us, because he could not solve
it himself.

Technically, one of the women was the man's *kit fat*, or
senior wife, while the other was really a concubine. But the

case had one curious feature. The first woman with whom the man had—to use one of the law's most graceless words—cohabited, was the concubine; and she had borne him a son. The man had then married the other woman as his *kit fat*, but she had had no son. Thus, in a certain sense, the two women could be regarded as equal in marital rank.

For some years the whole family had been living under one roof, and the husband, perplexed by the continual quarrels of his wives, had not been given a pleasant time. The wives had taken to enlisting the support of other women in the village, in which two parties had formed, causing disputes, and giving rise to scandal.

In addition to his house in the village, the husband had another smaller house in a hamlet situated in the hills above the village, and where he owned some additional fields. The village elder's opinion, with which I concurred, was that, in the interests of peace and public order in the village, one of the wives should be sent to live in the husband's second house, where he could regularly visit her.

The question was, which wife should be ordered to go?

The husband himself could not make the decision without rendering his life even more unendurable than it already was. Neither could the village elder, since whichever way he decided would put half the village against him. He had concluded that the decision must be made by an outsider, and imposed by authority. It was thus that he had brought them to the court.

The husband spent the greater part of his time in the main village, since, in addition to growing rice, he engaged in in-shore prawn fishing, using stake-nets.

In the ordinary way, the required decision would have

been a simple one. The *kit fat* would remain in the village house, the concubine move to the hamlet. But with the two wives virtually equal in status, the problem became more complicated.

Were I to order the concubine to move, there would be trouble over the son, who was still quite young. Strictly speaking, the *kit fat* could demand that the boy remain with her, even though she was not his actual mother. The father, not wishing to be separated from his son for the greater part of the year, would, in such an event, probably support his *kit fat*'s demand, resulting in the real mother being all but deprived of her own child.

The two wives were in a very bad temper, behaving almost as objectionably as the women in the calf case. They were both hard-workers, with the hard features that often go with rustic women who have had to work all their lives. Each on her own would probably have been a good wife, but together they were impossible.

Basically, beneath the hostile flow of their mutual accusations and recriminations, each wife was pursuing the same argument, and it boiled down to this: Why should I have to leave this man with that woman, who is unkind to him? And in fact, as I saw it, this question of kindness to the husband was the real crux of the matter. Decision should go in favour of the husband staying for the greater part of the year with whichever wife was the kinder of the two. At one point I made it fairly clear that this was my view, and was happy to see that the village elder agreed with me.

The village elder, of course, knew perfectly well which was the kinder wife, but could not possibly tell me. Somehow I had to find this out for myself. But with both wives hurling invective at each other, and occasionally at me as well, the quality of kindness was well concealed. There was even a moment when, roused myself by their aspersions, I told them roundly I didn't think there was a grain of kindness in either of them. This, of course—as usual, when the Special Magistrate came out with it—only made matters worse. Each wife savagely shouted at me that she was kind.

It went on and on, and I was nearing despair. It seemed ridiculous to be defeated by such an essentially simple matter. And then—I had not been conscious of the time, but it was one o'clock—suddenly the door burst open, and there was the noodle boy, clad in short pants and a singlet, grinning from ear to ear and holding aloft my lunch.

Unaware that the court was in session—with all the accusations flying about, it was difficult to tell it was a court—he swept in gaily, with a friendly greeting to me, came round to my side of the desk, laid the tray before me and with a sweeping gesture took the lid off the noodles.

A cloud of steam arose from the dish in the faces of the astonished wives; and the succulent odour of the incomparable noodles pervaded the court. Only just refraining from giving me a friendly pat on the back, the noodle boy thereupon sailed out of the room, taking the dish-cover with him.

There was nothing else for it. The noodles had to be eaten at once, or wasted. Besides, they smelt and looked extremely inviting.

"Now look, you people," I said, "this is a busy day for me, but I don't want to interrupt you. Just carry on telling me everything you want to say; I shall be listening. But will you please forgive me, all of you, if at the same time I have my lunch?"

While this was being interpreted, I removed the chopsticks from their enfolding napkin, and, just prior to embarking on the food, glanced up for a response.

The village elder was exchanging a smile with Mr. Lo. The husband was staring at me in blank amazement.

But it was the wives who drew my attention. The *kit fat*'s small round eyes were staring at me from out of her close-drawn skin with venom and unspeakable contempt. The concubine, on the contrary, for the first time since entering the room, broke into a charming smile, and said:

"Of *course*, Li Man Fu, sir, of *course* you must eat your noodles!"

We had discovered which of the two was the kinder, when it came to looking after a man.

I allowed the case to proceed for a little longer, in order to conceal from them that it had been decided, not by me, but by the noodles. Then I gave an order. The *kit fat* would move to the hamlet, where the husband would please be sure to visit her regularly; and both the husband and his concubine were enjoined to ensure that their son went to see his 'senior' mother as often as possible.

That this was the correct decision was evidenced, as correct decisions always were, by a sudden complete calm. It was as if no one had ever uttered a cross word. With perfect goodwill, they rose to leave. They had all known all along that this was the only sensible solution, but had needed someone in authority to tell them so. They had journeyed to the office for the express purpose of being given precisely this order, and they had received it. The business was at an end.

But the village elder's face was a study. His humorous eyes, smiling into mine, were saying:

'You were right, of course. But how in heaven's name did you find out?'

The particular point on which, at this hearing, the Special Magistrate outrivalled Solomon, was that he reached a decision equal in wisdom to Solomon's, but without having to threaten to carve a child in half.

That noodle-shop is excellent. I recommend it.

14

Seven Years in a Boat

SOLOMON, HOWEVER, WAS OCCASIONALLY defeated by circumstances. Nothing is more annoying than this.

A representative instance concerned a fishing couple, married for seven years and childless, who came to the court to obtain a divorce.

The man was what, in Cantonese slang, is called a Hoklo, meaning that he belonged to a wandering tribe of coastal and estuary fishermen, originally from Fukien province, and speaking a dialect of Fukienese. The Hoklo are to be found all along the southern coast of China, from Fukien province to Hainan Island. In this instance, the man spoke neither Cantonese nor Hakka, the two principal languages of the district, and no one in the office could understand his dialect.

Normally in China, when linguistic differences of this kind occur, matters are resolved in writing, the Chinese written language being universally understood, overriding dialectical differences to a degree sufficient to be comprehensible. Our Hoklo fisherman, unfortunately, was illiterate.

With some difficulty, Mr. Lo managed to find an educated Hoklo—there were not many at that time—who could interpret into Cantonese. There then remained the problem of the wife, who was from a rural district of Kwangsi province, hundreds of miles from Hongkong, and who insisted that she must have an interpreter who understood her language, since she too could not speak the languages of the district. To find someone speaking her particular brand of Chinese—she too was illiterate—proved an even harder problem; but we finally succeeded, and the case, with what seemed a somewhat massive array of people to assist, began.

Both husband and wife were delightful—sun-tanned, healthy, and straightforward in their manner. The husband was about thirty-five, lined for his years by constant exposure to the elements. The wife was a truly beautiful countrywoman, about the same age as her husband, buxom, even-complexioned, with a splendid bone-structure, and calm, even eyes betokening transparent honesty.

They sat before me with perfect patience, though it took a terribly long time to say anything. First, I would ask a question in English. This would be interpreted into Cantonese by Mr. Lo, then into Hoklo by the unofficial and very friendly Hoklo interpreter. The husband would then reply, his answer being transmitted through the same channel in reverse. To the wife I would ask a question in English, which would be interpreted into Cantonese by Mr. Lo, thence by someone else into a dialect of which I had never heard, thence by still one more person into the wife's own dialect, equally unheard-of; and the same laborious business in reverse.

There was no animosity between husband and wife. For seven years they had lived together in a small boat. The Hoklo are among the coastal people of China who seldom have houses ashore. If they feel a desire to live ashore, they simply drag their boat up the beach, and continue to live in it, but with a superstructural cabin added. They do not feel comfortable on flat floors. A Hoklo boat, not all that much larger than a sampan, is curved like a crescent moon. Moving in it is all ups and downs. This particular couple had lived entirely at sea, without superstructure, sleeping under mats through the heavy summer rains. Both were well-nourished, and in perfect physical condition. They usually frequented one of the smaller but more populous islands of the district, where there was a ready market for their fish.

Recently, the wife had told her husband she wished to return among her own people. He did not want her to leave him—they were clearly very attached to each other—but she had insisted. What did not have to be explained was that she considered she had let him down by not bearing him a child. She wished him to be free to take a second wife—impossible if she stayed in the boat—while perhaps, if she went back to her native Kwangsi, she might herself find another chance, before it was too late.

They were such a well-matched couple, each thinking only of the other, that I found it heartrending. I wondered if, even with these people who were not truly of the district, the magistrate's advice might be heeded. They had come to us, after all.

"You have told me you don't wish your wife to go," I said. "Why don't you ask her now to change her mind, and stay with you?"

Lengthily, through the interpreters, this went forth; and back came a strange answer:

"I can't."

"What d'you mean, you can't?" I asked him gently. "Ask her now, in front of me. Don't be shy. I believe she will change her mind."

Slowly and cumbersomely it went forth; and by the man's understanding expression, I could see it had reached him correctly. But back came the same answer:

"I can't."

As it was delivered to me, all the interpreters present began exchanging quiet queries and answers among themselves, and with both husband and wife. The matter resolved itself in a silence, in which I observed every interpreter suppressing a smile.

For seven years the couple had lived together in that small boat, and they had no common language.

I was shaking my head in silent wonder, when Mr. Lo's face burst into the most angelic smile I had ever seen it wear.

"Ah!" he sighed, with the sympathy of his experienced years. "The language of love!"

I looked at the husband and wife. Across the barriers of race and language, which seemed to lie like an eternity between us, each was looking at me with complete confidence that I would understand. Though we all lived to be a hundred, we would never be able to speak to one another; yet, in a sense, at that moment we did speak. Neither of them, I knew, would ever forget that moment; and neither would I.

"Mr. Lo, d'you think they were ever really married?"

After the usual passing to and fro, answer was given that they had not really been married.

"Then why—?" I began—and then I checked myself. They wished to do everything properly, to safeguard each other's future.

But it irked and upset me to do it.

"Seven years in a boat!" I murmured to Mr. Lo. "It's

such an achievement, it's a pity they can't carry on."

"I agree," he sighed. "But with all these interpreters, how shall we ever get it over to them?"

It was true; and with reluctance, I opened the huge leather-bound volume, and annulled the marriage that had never been performed.

15

A Case of Immaculate Conception

I CANNOT RESIST telling this one.

The court was rather more full than usual, most of the adult members of two families having come in. The two families were neighbours, living in a rather ramshackle, but fairly solid, row of wooden shop-houses in a congested part of industrial Tsuen Wan. Technically they were squatters, and the area was one of those we hoped eventually to see pulled down to make way for modern apartment blocks.

They were single-storey structures. In most of them, the shop section fronted the street; further in was the sleeping area, flimsily compartmented for various members of the family; after this came the kitchen and washing places, and a small rear yard, filled with the astonishing ragbag collections which Chinese of this type amass as some obscure part of their instinct for survival.

The complainant family had a daughter, aged about eighteen and still unmarried, who was in the unfortunate position of expecting a baby; and her parents had come to demand that I order the twenty-year-old son of the neighbouring family to marry their daughter without delay, since, they alleged, he was the unborn baby's father.

The defendant family said that this allegation was preposterous nonsense, that their son had never had anything to do with the girl, and that they refused to be browbeaten in this disgraceful way, their son accused of immorality.

203

There was no question of his marrying the girl, and there never had been. They scarcely knew their neighbours anyway, and their son had never even spoken to the girl.

The boy and the girl were present. Inhibited somewhat by their parents, who were doing most of the talking, they were both pleasant types. The boy worked in a factory; the girl worked at home making plastic handbags.

"Do you confirm what your father says, that you've never spoken to this girl?" I asked.

He confirmed it.

I turned to the girl's father.

"But you are suggesting that this is untrue," I said. "You are suggesting that your daughter has, in fact, spoken to this young man."

The girl's father was truculent. He didn't know whether his daughter had spoken to the boy or not. What he did know was that this was the young man who had interfered with his daughter.

"And are you saying, too, that you have never spoken to this young man?" I inquired of the girl.

She lowered her eyes, and would not reply.

"But you insist that he is the father of your baby?" I pursued.

She was silent for a long time. She had flushed, eyes always downcast.

"Yes," she whispered at last.

"Listen, young man," I said to the boy, "are you quite sure you're telling me the truth? Isn't there something else you *could* tell me, if your parents were not here— something you would prefer them not to know?"

Eyes downcast on his side too, his pale face gave no indication of a reaction. But my remarks produced a protest from his parents. Their son had nothing to conceal, they insisted. They knew the position. The other family's allegation was totally without foundation.

"Are you sure," I went on, addressing the boy, "that you haven't met this girl somewhere outside?"

"No! Of course he hasn't!" shouted both his parents simultaneously.

"No," replied the boy, quietly and quite plainly.

It sounded like the truth.

I addressed myself to the girl's father.

"I must tell you frankly, I find it difficult to deal with this complaint of yours. What you are saying about this young man is a very grave accusation. You cannot expect me to believe it, or even listen to it, unless you can produce some facts to substantiate it."

"I have facts!" he retorted hotly.

"Well—?"

"In the shower!" he snapped out.

"I beg your pardon?" I inquired, vaguely wondering where there might be a shower in our office.

"Yes," he said. "In the shower! That's where!"

I cupped my chin in my hands.

"What shower? Where?"

"In my house!"

"Oh! I understand!" I exclaimed; then, finding that I didn't, added, "No, I'm afraid I don't understand. What do you really mean?"

"When she takes a *shower*!" the wretched father shouted at me, almost overcome by my inability to understand.

"When she takes a shower," I repeated slowly. "Where *is* the shower?"

From my office one was always distantly aware of the bustle and noise in the other parts of the building; and at this moment I wondered why it was that I should have suddenly thought about this. Then it occurred to me. There were surprisingly few sounds from the rest of the building. There was, in fact—apart from the distant bustle of Kowloon—almost silence. There was, now I came to pay keener attention to the matter, more than silence. There was what is known behind the scenes in the London theatre as 'deathly hush', which is a kind of indrawing of breath (accompanied by tiptoes and craned heads) so absolutely silent as to be painfully audible.

I did not have to be told. All work in the outer offices had stopped, while every member of the staff who considered himself sufficiently senior to do so had silently crept up the passage, where, just out of sight from the open door of my office, the lot of them had assembled, poised, listening to every word with bated breath.

"Where is the shower?" I repeated steadily, trying hard to control myself from yelling at the staff to go back to their work.

The shower, it appeared, was at the back of the house. With a projecting cover of some sort, it was external to the building, situated in the back yard, and modestly screened.

"You mean," I said, "that it is possible to pass from your back yard to your neighbour's?"

Certainly not! came the almost injured reply. There was a strong plank wall between the two yards, and it was impossible to pass.

"Then what do you mean? Where does the shower come into it?"

"He *saw* her!" the girl's father shouted at me desperately.

"I see. You mean, realizing she was having a shower, he managed to climb over the plank wall, and . . ." Modesty forbade the rest.

But the poor father only looked more desperate than ever.

"He *saw* her!" he repeated, with even greater emphasis.

This was becoming too much for the Special Magistrate.

"Look here, my dear man," I said reasoningly, "you are not, I hope, trying to tell me that if a young man chances to see a young girl having a shower, this causes the girl to make a baby. Or are you?"

From the youngsters there was silence. From the four parents there was a unanimous snort of disgust at finding they had journeyed all this way to be heard by a magistrate who asked such ridiculous questions.

"*He* doesn't understand," the father muttered contemptuously to my interpreter, using an off-hand word to describe me.

"No, he certainly doesn't!" I replied sharply, before the interpreter had time to translate. "If you have a genuine grievance against this family, or against this young man, why do you not tell me what it is?"

It seemed to me that their accusation against the boy was a cover, shielding the real cause of their animosity towards the other family. This real cause was evidently something quite different. But how to discover what it was?

There was silence.

"Well, I'm sorry," I said, "but if that is all you can produce to substantiate your statement I'm afraid my answer must be that this young man has no case to answer."

With triumphant looks and inaudible sniffs, the boy's parents turned their backs on the other parents, who remained silent, the girl's father staring at me with the helplessness an intelligent man evinces when trying to explain something to an ignoramus.

"Listen to me," I said to him, by this time almost in my own self-defence. "You have all more or less agreed that this young man has never spoken to your daughter. He may once have seen her taking her bath—perhaps you should make that plank wall higher. Your daughter must go out sometimes on her own. How do you know that she doesn't have some other boy friend, whom you know nothing about?"

They dismissed this out of hand. Their daughter did not go out on her own.

"Then, what you are telling me is that this young man, by having set eyes on your daughter when she was naked, has caused her to conceive a child."

All of them rustled about for a moment—Western magistrates, it seemed to them, had strange ideas—and then the girl's father muttered under his breath to the interpreter:

"Can't he understand? At *night*!"

"At night?" I queried. "You mean, your daughter is in the habit of taking a shower at night?"

In the passage outside, there was a sudden renewed outburst of deathly hush. It evidenced the fact that the only person in the office who did *not* know what this case was about was the Special Magistrate, the game being to see how long it would take him to find out. They may even have been laying bets on it.

No, certainly not! came the reply to my query. The girl did *not* take a bath at night.

"Then what has night got to do with it?" I asked. "Where *are* you all usually at night? Sleeping, I presume."

Yes. They were sleeping.

"Well, where do you sleep?"

It appeared that the sleeping quarters in both houses were approximately adjacent, that both front and back doors were securely locked before everyone went to sleep, and that there was no possibility of anyone passing from one house to the other, or going outside, without waking someone up.

I had reached the end of this line of questioning, and it had led nowhere. But being for the moment at a loss to know what to ask them next, and being unwilling to show them I was lost, with wearied obstinacy I pursued the same line a little further, all the while thinking hard what really salient question to raise next.

"And where exactly do you sleep?" I asked the girl in a bored way.

She slept in the same bed as her mother.

"And where do you sleep?" I inquired of the boy.

He slept alone.

It was meaningless to pursue the matter, but I went on listlessly.

"Whereabouts do you have your bed?"

His bed was against the wall.

"Which wall?"

It was the wall of the other shop-house.

The deathly hush in the passage suddenly became so strident that it could have been called screaming deathly hush. It appeared I was on to something.

I addressed the girl's mother.

"And just where is your bed situated?"

Her bed too was against a wall—the wall of the other shop-house.

"And you say your daughter shares your bed with you?"

"Yes."

"Which—er"—it was difficult to know how to word it—"which of you sleeps on the room side of your bed?"

"I do," the mother replied.

"I see. So your daughter sleeps on the wall side?"

"Yes."

The wall was of wood, and perhaps a knotch had fallen out of it. Anyway, somewhere—and at just about the right place—there was a hole in it.

Not a very big hole. But just big enough.

This case occurred in my third year as a magistrate, when I should have known better than to have kept those six people in such prolonged embarrassment. I say all six were embarrassed, because, as the reader, who is by this time becoming accustomed to the happenings in a Chinese court, will already have realized, the boy's parents, despite the attitudes they struck, were fully aware of what had happened. There was even a moment (when they swung themselves away from the other parents) when they thought that, with such an idiot of a magistrate, they were going to get away with it—because they did not really wish their son to marry, considering him to be too young.

Perhaps it was particularly hot and humid that morning—I can't remember—but anyway, I was extremely slow in the uptake, since I was not paying attention to the euphemisms being employed. In no language is euphemism used more than in Chinese, and on no subject are there more Chinese euphemisms than in anything pertaining to sex. Coarsenesses apart—and the Chinese language has its fair share of these—it would almost be true to say that sex, if it is ever mentioned at all in speech, can only be mentioned in euphemistic terms. The very word for sex—the secret thing—is a euphemism.

In what the girl's father was saying to me, the shower in the back yard had nothing to do with it. For 'shower' read 'naked', for 'saw' read 'touched', and it will be seen that the father was making a completely explicit statement: 'When she was naked, he touched her in the night.' He could not be more explicit without using unprintable words.

And there the six of them had sat, in acute embarrassment, because for some reason that morning I was too slow-witted to grasp it.

This is a story which, I think, gives an idea of the difficulties involved in understanding what goes on around one in a Chinese society. To appreciate how silly a foreigner can be in China, it is almost worth glancing at the dialogue of the case a second time, this time suffering with the two Chinese families, instead of struggling with the magistrate.

But to the reader who wishes to do this, let me first explain why they had come. What had happened was too shameful for the boy's parents to admit—the entire family would have lost face—and this had created a socially impossible situation, which the two families themselves could not resolve, and which could *never* be the basis of a marriage alliance. Once again, as with the case in which the magistrate outrivalled the wisdom of Solomon, authority was needed to put things right.

Very gently and kindly, the Special Magistrate inquired of the young couple whether they would like to start talking to each other—because it was true, they never had—and Mr. Lo, reading my meaning from my tone of voice, skilfully slipped my words into the perfect Chinese euphemism, behind which lay the implication, 'Would you like to get married?'

Both smiled, and said they would; and the suggestion having come from so exalted a source, all question of shame was removed.

They all departed in a comparatively amiable state—I say comparatively, because none of the four parents had really yet recovered from the shock of discovering that they had produced offspring of quite such exceptional agility.

16

The District and the World

AS I MENTIONED at the beginning, life in Hongkong could be said to be lived in two dimensions: Hongkong's own small dimension, in which local matters loom large; and the large dimension of things seen in relation to China and the continent of Asia, in which local matters appear to be exceedingly small.

In that larger dimension, those were grave, forbidding years. Internal communist insurrections gripped the Philippines and Malaya. Indonesia, already a closed country, was drifting steadily into communism; Burma was much the same. In Ceylon, the political extreme left was threatening the country's future, while India had embarked on her suicidal political flirtation with China. The spread of communism to all Korea had been stemmed, but in a war of appalling slaughter. The French were fighting a losing war against communism in Indo-China. Much in Asia pointed to the possibility of the entire continent being stifled beneath the communist shroud.

It may be asked whether, on its small scale, the district reflected any of the greater happenings going on around it, and whether it posed any object-lessons applicable to them. Inevitably it did, though it was quite easy to pass them by without noticing them.

Let me now attempt to fuse the two dimensions, and, from actions in the smaller, seek conclusions concerning the greater. This, of course, will be presumptuous; arguing from the particular to the general nearly always is. But to observe whether, and if so in what, a dot on the map reflects an immense continent, has a certain intrinsic interest. Besides, in these pages the small dimension has predominated; and unless the larger dimension, in which it dwelt, is recalled to mind, the balance will not be just.

Fusing the two dimensions, therefore, I will speak, on the smaller, of my own small doings in my district, and, on the larger, of three things that commanded the attention of the times: communism, negotiation with China, and aid to underdeveloped countries.

It was widely said at that time—and it still is—that communism breeds on poverty. One of the motives for the United States' massive aid to poorer countries stemmed from the belief that to eradicate poverty would halt the spread of communism.

In the district, I saw a good deal of communism, and from an angle and at a stage which people do not often think about—at the point of individual inception in the mind of a boy or a girl.

The scene is a village within reasonably easy distance of the city. Though life in the village is simple, it is a prosperous place; no one there has ever known what real hunger is, and people have all their needs. No one reads books, though most of the men can read and write; occasionally someone comes home from town with a newspaper, which subsequently drifts from house to house.

For an intelligent boy—and communism has little appeal to those who are not intelligent—the village is a place of despair. It is doomed to be inferior in relation to the city, and so is anyone who is born there, unless he can acquire the learning of the city. The only future lies in the city, but coming from the village one begins with a permanent handicap.

The teachers at the nearby middle school, well educated and respectable people, teach civics, and do not see things in terms of town and country. The school books have all been written by people who presumably live in cities; most of what the books contain concerns cities. And where are the teachers themselves at the weekend? In the city. They return to the country very early on Monday mornings, jointly sharing a taxi.

Then comes a new teacher, who visits people in their houses, helps the people to build a basketball court at the middle school, and who, instead of going to the city at weekends, takes selected boys to visit other villages, or teaches them to swim, or hires a boat and takes them fishing, and in whatever he does treats the boys as adults.

This teacher is a communist; and his presence among the boys *compensates* them for their subconscious feeling of inferiority. He speaks little or nothing of politics. His presence among the boys, and his manner of life, reveal to them that there is a purpose in life, which no one in the village understands. That purpose begins by meaning to help others, but it gradually changes, until it comes to mean standing together; and when this stage has been reached, some simple political instruction can be given. The boy who falls for this now believes himself dedicated to a purpose. Actually, he has merely become secretly aloof from his own folk.

Once the teacher has made his selection, he is as protective of his flock as a Catholic nun with girls in a convent. The presence of communism in a school can be sensed at the instant of crossing the threshold. The teacher is polite and respectful, but no direct exchange with the students is possible; it might contaminate them. The teacher declines my invitation to lunch, and when obliged to meet me socially in a restaurant, pointedly sips a soft drink, when I have ordered beer. His is a dedicated life; mine, it would seem, is not.

The point which he has touched in those boys, and which is the foundation of the communist cell, is the desire of youth for self-sacrifice, which till then has been thwarted by circumstances. I have never been able to understand what people mean when they say that communism breeds on poverty. Communism's breeding-ground seems to me to have nothing whatever to do with poverty. The seed of communism in a man's heart is his subconscious sense of inferiority; and it most readily germinates, so far as young people are concerned, when for any one of a multitude of reasons subconscious inferiority comes into conjunction with youthful desire for self-sacrifice which can find no outlet. The boy who has received less favour than his brother, the girl who fears she is not pretty, the man who, left on his own, feels himself threatened, these are the people I have watched become communist. All of them had enough to eat, and so did those around them.

In the countryside it was often the more intelligent and interesting boys who were the first to be influenced, since in them the subconscious sense of inferiority (to the city) was more acute. Where communist influence can be detected at a sufficiently early age, the most useful thing that anyone in authority can do is to put such a young man in the way of a job, or find some other means of getting him into a position of responsibility.

In Hongkong, and later in South-East Asia, I had the good fortune to be able to deal with a number of potentially dangerous young men—dangerous to a free society—

in this way, often without their knowing it; and all of them turned out to be unusually reliable citizens.

One, in South-East Asia, I particularly remember. He was a Chinese student, and there was no material assistance I could give him; but I occasionally invited him to my house, when others were present and public affairs were discussed, and I also sometimes included him in my excursion parties.

In this way, he saw with his own eyes what governmental responsibility is, without my having to teach him anything. Communism was never once mentioned. It was only instinct that led me to believe that, in his school, he was on his way to becoming a communist youth leader, or might already have become one; and I often wondered whether my concern about him was misplaced.

Some years later, there was a communist insurrection in his country, which I was then visiting. My student friend by this time had a university degree and was holding a responsible government position. One day, when we were out in the country, he nodded in the direction of the communist-held jungle, and said, "Had it not been for you, I would now be out there."

With the schoolteacher the situation was different, because he was already a ticket-holder. Nevertheless, I always believed in working on much the same principle as with the student. In a free society, when the police say, 'Beware of that man; he's a communist', it is the natural tendency of a government official to steer clear of him. My opinion is that, on the contrary, it is better to associate with him, even though it may mean—as frequently happened to me, I should add—attracting police suspicion to oneself.

Whenever I found a communist teacher in the district, I

would, wherever possible, go out of my way to associate such a man with what I was doing, and, in particular, take him with me when I was touring, in the hope that, despite his convictions, he might perceive (as the student did) how complex government is, how difficult it is to reconcile clashing interests, and that, in sum, no government can function (not even a communist one, when it comes to it) on the basis of a theory.

No theory in government is absolute, not even the theory of right and wrong, since what is right for one set of people is nearly always wrong for another. As to the ethics of government, there is only one ethic, and that is restraint. As the Chinese philosopher Lao Tze wisely wrote, 'Rule a great empire as you would cook a small fish'—meaning, don't overdo it.

In the district I had to conduct many negotiations with Chinese people—commercial negotiations, usually involving land, and political negotiations, some with communist organizations; others—more complicated—were with local power groups. Some of these negotiations were by no means easy, and had it not proved possible to bring them to agreeable conclusions, some of them would have led to public disorder, and to the imposition of government orders by force—the mark of failure.

These negotiations taught me a number of things, some of which—stepping once more from the smaller to the larger dimension—I believe to be relevant to the greater general question of negotiation with China.

A Chinese negotiation differs from negotiation elsewhere in two respects: in its indirectness, and in what may be termed a margin of indefiniteness.

The degree of indirectness required in a Chinese negotiation is something which is apt to reduce any but the most patient Westerner to exasperation. Everything, from start to finish and at all levels, must be done indirectly, to avoid all possibility of any kind of confrontation or show-down. No contrary word should be uttered except to a third party, who will transmit it in his own way—often, be it added, in a wrong sense, which has subsequently to be rectified by similar indirect methods.

It is all but useless for a negotiator, whether diplomatic or commercial, to go to China and expect to discuss matters with his opposite number. Negotiation is the work of underlings, who on the Chinese side will be provided. If the Western negotiator arrives without underlings of his own, he has instantly lost his status.

The very last thing that a negotiator is expected to do in China is to negotiate. The duty of the principal person in a negotiation is to meet his opposite number, engage him in delightful dinner parties and pleasant country excursions, give well-chosen presents to his hosts and hostesses, and be amiable. The perfectly conducted negotiation is one in which neither of the principal persons concerned ever has to refer to the matter in hand.

This may sound like something out of an antique fairy tale, but it is not. It is China as it was, as it is, and as it will be. The Chinese dislike of direct confrontations is exceedingly deep, pervading Chinese life from begin-ning to end. A Westerner who reckons without it will get nowhere.

To take an absurdly small example of how it works, there was a time when my cook was not making bacon and eggs in quite the way I like them. I did not dare tell him so, since this, in its very small way, would have been a confrontation. Instead, I telephoned his 'back mountain', the man who years earlier had recommended him to me, and said, "Please ask him not to overcook the bacon." The speed with which this message was transmitted was reflected in the bacon and eggs next day being entirely to satisfaction. As he brought them in, my cook gave me a knowing look and was happy, because the matter had been conducted in a proper way. Never a word was said.

Six months living with a Chinese family is, I reckon, just about the time required to ensure that the unprepared Westerner will end in a mental institution. Matters which, in the West, would be settled by a three-minute telephone call and prompt delivery of the goods, in a Chinese family often take hours, days, weeks to achieve, while the family try one go-between, who turns out to be the wrong one, then try someone else, then give up hope for a week, and then suddenly think of the right person, and the matter is settled in minutes.

Life in the family house is delightful; everything is beautifully run; the food is marvellous; and people are considerate of one another to a truly remarkable degree. The outcome, in other words, is the same as in a Western home—in some ways better—but the mechanics by which this is achieved are entirely different. Matters which in the West would take a long time to fix are resolved on the instant. You never know what to expect. All you have to remember, as a Westerner, is to be patient. Family dramas which in the West would set any family into commotion—such as the eldest son running away with a call-girl—will be received with such complete calm (because the family are doing something about it in their own way) that you would never know anything was wrong. Then one day you will hear the whole house in uproar, and wonder what on earth is the matter, only to discover that father has come home

8—MAM

with mud on his trousers, having been sprayed by a passing car.

Staying in a Chinese home—this is a digression, but it may perhaps help to illustrate the main point—nothing will be explained to you, and you must learn never on any account to ask questions, even the simplest ones, since propriety in matters of conversation is yet another matter which differs entirely from the West.

Hilarious and ribald conversations, in which even grand-mother will participate, will be held on subjects which in the West would be enough to reduce any dinner-table to stunned silence. Yet a simple inquiry—about a member of the family, perhaps, and which in the West would be considered thoughtful and polite—may easily prove to be indelicate, and cause embarrassment.

One of the difficulties here is that Chinese take it for granted that nothing is said without a motive; and thus, if a motive is not at once apparent (the Western motive simply being to say something polite), it will set people thinking, wondering what you are really up to.

In the West, though most of us are unconscious of this, we say many things without a motive, it often being polite to do so. In the West, for example, we say, 'I hope you are well', when it has never occurred to us to hope either one way or the other; we have simply said it 'in a manner of speaking'—a phrase which to Chinese is very revealing of the West, since it implies insincerity. In China you do not say things 'in a manner of speaking'. You either say, or you do not say. And where we say, 'I hope you are well', Chinese say 'Are you well?'—in which case, if they hope you are not, at least they have not had to say they hope you are.

It is from such small points that the angles between

China and the West widen into great differences, and into much misunderstanding. To use the same illustration, to say 'I hope you are well' in Chinese has such a strange ring about it, that it would instantly be deduced you hoped the exact opposite. Thus, as a Westerner arriving in China, even when shaking hands with someone, you have to remember where you are. Nothing—*nothing*—is as it would seem.

The other unusual aspect of a Chinese negotiation is the margin of indefiniteness which must always be left at the end of it.

Earlier on, discussing religion, and again discussing geomancy, just when it seemed that the moment was drawing near when the absolute fundamentals of Chinese belief would be revealed, it was found that these were situated in the empty spaces between two Western words, and could not be brought within the tactile grasp.

This is so true of China, when it comes to submitting things to Western analysis, that it could perhaps be called the most important point of all. I have many times said privately that the only sure way of discussing the deepest aspects of Chinese philosophy and life is after a little liquor, and in pidgin English. The liquor allows for inexactitudes, while pidgin English, albeit rigidly exact, has between each word those merciful interstices of indefiniteness, without taking account of which, and without recognizing as being *permanent* interstices—sheer blank space—China cannot be understood, far less enjoyed.

Here the difficulty is that the Western mind simply will not leave such blank spaces alone. What is *in* them, people ask? How *can* there be such a thing as a blank space in the thinking of an entire civilization?

There is a blind spot in everyone's eye. When it is

brought to anyone's attention, the fact is recognized. But what do you see when you try to look through it? And what advantage is there in trying?

The point is that, despite its blind spot, the eye is a perfect organ of the human body. So, too, is it with the Chinese interstices. They are not a deficiency. The thought and reasoning in Chinese civilization are complete. It is simply that there are certain points on which Chinese thought remains deliberately indefinite; and to seek to define what is there in those interstices is as foolish as to try to see through the blind spot in your own eye.

This factor of the indefinite has a most important relevance to negotiation, as well as to manners, the making of arrangements, and many other things. The Western insistence on obtaining exact facts, making precise definitions and drawing absolute conclusions, breaks down in China somewhere between ninety-five and ninety-eight in the hundred degrees. A Westerner who persists in demanding exactitudes after ninety-five is a bore, after ninety-eight rude. Contracts, oaths, sworn statements, and suchlike are other features of the West which can never be more than 95 per cent respected in China—if that—since they deal with absolutes; and to the Chinese mind, the absolute is essentially absurd, because it does not exist.

The West, with its transcendentalism, dogma, anathema, and similar concepts, will not accept the truth of this. The West instinctively *seeks* absolutes, *desires* them. Its philosophical books reek of them, and to the Chinese mind are consequently indescribably dull, since the philosophers are dealing with what they should surely have realized before they started was *unreal*, as Chinese see it.

Similarly, in the West, people desire a perfect car, a perfect servant, a perfect house, all of which denotes the same striving for the impossible, and is—when one comes to think of it—ridiculous. If one can arrange matters 90 per cent to satisfaction, one can already consider oneself extremely fortunate. After that, relax. What happens if you fill a glass 100 per cent full? The wine spills on the table-cloth. Even in the West, it is recognized that a wineglass should not be more than about 90 per cent full. In China a wineglass should be filled 98 per cent, with the meniscus just reaching to the brim. 98 per cent, in other words, means full.

Ah! the Western mind exclaims. What you are actually recommending is a policy of *laisser-aller*, the thin end of the wedge, agreements that need not be scrupulously adhered to.

When an agreement is scrupulously adhered to, it is because of the *character* of those who have agreed to it, and the degree of understanding that exists between them. It is not because of the written contract, which, when it comes to it, is merely a reminder of the points that have been previously agreed to. It is this element of *character*, which throughout the Orient is the most important of all criteria of judgment, which might in a sense—and here I succumb to my own Western dislike of blank spaces—be said to lie in those subtle interstices of indefiniteness.

Because of this element in Chinese thinking—the element that has no time for absolutes—a Westerner has to be careful not to press too hard or too far in negotiation. The Western technique of making extreme demands, then moderating them, until an agreed balance is reached, is of course fatal in China. Moderate a demand, and you lose face. In a negotiation, the moment reached when you have created the position in which you can make demands, have in mind clearly what you want, and demand 70 per cent of it. In most instances, the next 25 per cent beyond this will be understood by the other side, and thus can by gentle steps be gained. The last 5 per cent is sacrosanct.

I remember once being sent into another country to conduct a Chinese negotiation, and having with me a European colleague unfamiliar with the Orient. I spent more time arguing with him than with the people we had been sent to negotiate with. He simply could not understand why, at a Chinese dinner, when we had our host perfectly poised in the position wherein we could make our final demand, I would deflect the conversation into some channel of frivolity and let the opportunity pass. Returned to our hotel, my colleague would be furious with me. Had I no sense of responsibility?

I tried to explain to him that, had we pressed our advantage, we would have ruined the dinner party, and by bringing matters to complete definiteness—the one thing at all costs to be avoided—would have soured up the entire course of the negotiation, besides giving our hosts a poor impression of our *character* as negotiators.

He never understood me; and when we finally left, with various points still undecided, he did not know what to make of it, complaining afterwards that we could have struck a far harder bargain, had I not so consistently bungled matters.

Indeed, we could have struck a far harder bargain. But Westerners who strike hard bargains do not last long in the Orient. In the nineteenth century, the nations of Europe struck hard bargains with China, made exact demands, and got everything they wanted. By the 'unequal treaties', China was humiliated. The humiliation, however, did not lie in the fact that the West was strong. That, with a hard swallow, could have been tolerated. The humiliation was that China was dictated to by people who behaved like boors.

Moreover, what was the outcome? Where are all those treaty ports and special concessions today? Losses such as Europe has suffered in China exemplify what will always happen if Chinese are pressed too hard.

An agreeably concluded negotiation can leave many things unsettled; and in all negotiation, something should always be left uncertain, to be decided by goodwill. This also leaves matters open to revision in the event of possible future ill-will, which is useful. Francis Bacon put much the same thing in a different way when he wrote, 'Love as if you were sometime to hate, and hate as if you were sometime to love.'

Finally, in a diplomatic or governmental negotiation, in which the Western negotiator will naturally have his own principles of proceeding, it is important never to forget the principles which will be guiding matters on the Chinese side. There will probably be no visible signs of it, but the Chinese officials will almost surely be sticking closely to their own maxim of the three principles, or duties, of sound government. These are:

> to simulate friendship;
> to express honeyed sentiments; and
> to treat your inferiors as your equals.

Thus when a diplomat in China—or indeed any Westerner engaged in formal business—finds himself being treated on terms of delightful equality, let him be on his guard; he is almost certainly being used for some ulterior purpose. The ambassador of the most powerful nation, with nuclear warheads and other mighty armament, is basically, from the instant of setting foot on the soil of China, and despite everything that may suggest the contrary, just another foreigner, i.e. inferior to the humblest farmer or shop assistant. A foreigner in China *is* inferior. He is inferior because more than 700,000,000 people all around him think so. There is no argument about it.

Then surely, it will be asked, it must be impossible to make true friends. Strangely enough, this is not so. As anyone who has lived among Chinese people will testify, Chinese friendship, once established, is of the truest.

But, in China, who *are* your friends? Your friends are those who have come to know and esteem you sufficiently to enable them to forgive, but not overlook, the fact that you are a foreigner. They are those who are aware that you are genuinely trying to behave properly, according to Chinese canons, and who, though they will be embarrassed, are prepared to forgive you when you unintentionally say or do something indelicate or indiscreet. On their side, they are in addition people with sufficient courage of their convictions not to mind being seen with you in public, since it should be remembered that in normal Chinese society, to be seen with foreigners is lowering.

The Chinese top-level, Westernized segment of society particularly demonstrates this quality of social courage, looking as they often do beyond the frontiers of China, and seeing things in a wider perspective. But when it comes to it, they too none the less regard themselves as innately superior, as you quickly discover if you accidentally rub them up the wrong way.

I was once in conversation with one of Europe's most eminent sinologues. He was married to a Chinese lady from a family of high standing, and I happened to know that the sinologue was *bien vu* by his Chinese in-laws. He thus seemed to be the right person of whom to ask a question, about which I had long wondered, namely, surely the circumstances—albeit rare ones—must exist in which a Chinese is capable of regarding a foreigner as a brother?

He thought for quite a long time, then nodded, and said:

"As a younger brother, yes."

To the reader familiar with China and the Chinese, all of this will seem very old stuff; but it will be agreed, I believe, that these are things that need to be stated and re-stated, since without taking them into account, no real understanding between China and the West will ever be possible.

The world is changing so quickly, its nations and races are drawing so markedly closer to one another in understanding, and in their material desires, that each year it becomes progressively more difficult to take in the fact that similar changes are not taking place among the Chinese, even in non-communist Chinese society. The Chinese do change—they have changed immeasurably since the turn of the century, and a great deal in even the past twenty years. But these changes are changes occurring within the orbit of Chinese civilization, which is distinct and separate, having, as was seen in the illustration of the Chinese family home, a different mechanism.

Within their own society, in other words, there is continual change; but in all that pertains to relations between a Chinese and a member of another race, there has been no change of any real significance; and this is something which has to be remembered by anyone who engages in the conduct of a Chinese negotiation.

A Cantonese friend of mine—and this is referring to Kwangtung, the dictionary—once explained the matter to me thus: the traditional Chinese psychological reaction to a foreigner is, firstly, not to hurt him, and secondly, to remember he is an enemy. The reason for not hurting him is the same as for not hurting animals; and, to give the completing touch to the complexity of it all, it has to be remembered that the very word for 'foreigner' in Chinese, when written down, has beside it the radical strokes denoting the genus 'animal'.

Foreign aid, mainly American, to underdeveloped countries has been a great feature of the decades since the Second World War. One of the most altruistic and selfless actions ever taken in history, to the dismay of many Americans, aid has been very widely misunderstood in the recipient countries, where its motive has frequently been misinterpreted as being one of cunning self-interest.

Withdrawing now from the larger dimension to the smaller one, let me tell a story from the district.

One late afternoon towards autumn, still in the period of the rains, I was returning by launch to the small island where I had a house, when it unexpectedly began to rain with such intensity that visibility was reduced to a few yards. The launch carrying no navigational instruments, since these were not normally required, the coxswain sent a message down from the bridge asking if I would mind if we stopped for a few minutes, since it was impossible to see where we were going. After about twelve minutes the sky cleared a little and we resumed our journey.

But when we rounded the point of the island, and entered the normally busy fishing port, we found it a scene of desolation. While we had been experiencing that unusually intense rain, on the island there had been an occurrence of a very rare gust of wind, which comes when the south wind of summer veers to the west, and then, abnormally reaching the north-west, gives a sudden flick, causing this particular wind to be known in Chinese as the dragon's tail.

For two terrible minutes this wind had blown, with such ferocity that, as the wife of the police officer told me afterwards, every pane of glass in her windows bulged inwards, and she herself hid under a bed.

Nearly every boat in the harbour had been overturned; and along the waterfront, beneath a black and angry sky, a crowd of Chinese stood staring at the scene in mute shock. Others had manned small boats, and were dragging people out of the water.

As I disembarked, from the other side of the pier one of the members of the island committee, his face wan and distraught, came up carrying the body of a dead child. We exchanged an anguished look, as also with others whom I knew in the crowd, after which I left the waterfront, walked through the town, and mounted the hill to my house.

From the hospital and the police station, the details gradually became known. Three huge ocean-going junks had sunk, thirty-seven smaller craft (every one of them the home of those who manned it) had capsized, seventy people had been admitted to hospital, and there were fourteen known dead.

Towards dusk I received a visit from a young and energetic Chinese friend of mine, a Hongkong government official born and brought up in the United States. He looked at me in consternation.

"What are you doing here?" he asked. "Don't you realize this is the worst disaster that's ever hit this island?"

I said I was well aware of it.

"Well, why don't you *do* something?" he said. "The people want help. It's your responsibility."

I replied that I was aware of that too.

"Well, what are you going to do?" he asked.

"Nothing," I replied.

He shook his head despairingly.

"I just don't understand you," he said. "Surely you could at least go down to the town, and show the people you appreciate what's happened?"

"No," I replied. "I shall stay here."

"I think you're completely cold-blooded," he said with another shake of the head, and left.

Down in the town, as I saw it, it would be a time of mourning and despair; and the last thing, I always believe, that Chinese desire on such occasions is the presence of a foreigner, expressing condolence and sympathy at the wrong moments and in the wrong way, adding a jarring element to an hour in which anguish must run its course.

Next day was a public holiday, and I was able to remain at home. Mid-morning my friend again came up to see me.

"*Surely* you're going to do something now?" he said urgently.

"No," I replied. "I'm doing nothing."

"But the whole town is asking what you're doing. They're asking why the government isn't helping them."

"I can't help that," I said. "I'm doing nothing."

He shrugged his shoulders at my callousness, and again left me; and I will confess that this time he had me worried. I wondered whether I had made an unwise decision.

Then, at three in the afternoon, up came the chairman and vice-chairman of the committee, with three senior members, all well known to me. They explained the seriousness of the disaster. Somehow the boats had to be refitted and enabled to go to sea, but the money required for this was far beyond the committee's resources. They gave me a figure which they thought the committee could afford, and an estimate of what they considered was actually required. Could I make any suggestion how this larger sum could be raised?

"Well," I said tentatively, "the first thing that strikes me is that no one outside the island knows yet that this disaster has happened. Would it be an idea if we went down now to the police station, asked to use their telephone, and informed the press? You could tell the Chinese newspapers; I will tell the English ones. Then, would you like me to launch a public appeal for funds?"

There was an almost audible sigh of relief from all of them, and we set off forthwith. That evening I went in to Hongkong and obtained permission to launch an appeal.

Next morning, the disaster was given prominent coverage in every paper, as was the appeal; and, as always on such occasions, the public response was generous and immediate. Beginning with a munificent personal donation by the Governor (who, as a young officer, spent his honeymoon on the island), money poured in all day, and by closing time we had many thousand dollars more than were actually required.

Meanwhile two teams of investigators, made up jointly of committee members and the island's government officials, took an inventory from every fishing family of exactly what they had lost, and estimated what each family would need for refitting. The following day these sums were distributed—plus a substantial grant to each family which had lost a life—the fishermen quickly purchased their needs in the island's well-provisioned shops, and in a matter of hours every boat was once more seaworthy.

Had this incident occurred in the West, what I should properly have done would have, of course, been exactly as my American Chinese friend had urged. I should have gone in at once among the people, extended sympathy, and taken immediate measures to organize relief. Had the disaster occurred where it did, but had I been Chinese, I might have done something along these lines, I might not. I simply do not know what would have been correct. But being a European, there seemed to me to be no alternative.

Had I gone down and organized relief, the committee would initially have been very thankful, but it would not have lasted. There is something overwhelming about Westerners on occasions of this kind. The speed with which they think things out, and the efficiency with which they get things done, reduce Chinese—and I have seen this happen many times—to a kind of temporary paralysis of thought and action.

What would have happened if I had taken the lead is that, after a few hours, the committee would have washed their hands of the matter, saying in substance, 'Leave it to the Li Man Fu; he's handling it.'

This would have meant engaging special temporary staff, at public expense, and appealing for local volunteers—who might not have volunteered to serve under European leadership in what was an exclusively Chinese affair. Also, the least mistake or delay, and the government would have been blamed.

As it was, the full brunt of responsibility fell on the committee. They examined their finances, thought the thing out properly, and then made the effort of climbing up the hill as a deputation and asking for advice. Thus, the subsequent publicity, and the appeal, were all direct results of their own activity; the inventories of requirements were made by people with thorough understanding of fishermen and their wants; and when, in the outcome, things far exceeded expectations, the committee felt proud of what they had done, and indeed received the congratulations of the whole town—all very satisfactory.

The incident shows—but in no more than a minor sense—the danger that exists, where the West is concerned, in accepting too readily the advice of Western-educated Asians, who are often, without anyone realizing it, out of touch with the reactions and desires of their own people. To Western ears their words sound sensible and convincing; but they are often words that are not quite Oriental, and to this extent can prove a trap to the unwary.

The age of aid seems at the present time to be passing, but it is doubtful whether it will ever pass away entirely; thus perhaps this small story may still be apposite. The West, with its speed and efficiency, and its bold, clear lines of action, is apt to be overwhelming in the Orient, where things must be done in an Oriental way if they are to prove successful.

Inevitably, Western aid has involved Western analysis of the economic and other weaknesses of various countries, followed by measures to remedy them; and this has given the impression that aid has been thrust upon countries, the West having an urgency about what it does which the Orient does not have. It is for this reason that the West's motive has been suspected.

To avoid misunderstandings, it is often wiser to make no positive moves (as I refrained from doing in this instance) to provide aid, merely letting it indirectly be known (as I did by remaining on the island) that the possibility of aid exists. In this way, people think out their own schemes, work out what they need and what they can afford, make the effort to obtain aid, and when the outcome is satisfactory, feel proud and happy. When this happens, too, there is a greater likelihood of the donated money being properly spent.

I will admit, however, that on that particular occasion, and on that particular island, I did not like doing it.

17

Mandate Surrendered

THE SPECIAL MAGISTRATE'S DAYS in the district were
brought to an end by overwork—and I admit this with no
pride, since while to work hard is good, to work too hard is
a misjudgment.

Night after night, and for weeks on end, it was the same.
I would retire to bed around 11.15 p.m. or so, and sleep
luxuriantly. I would awaken while it was still dark—as I
usually do—feeling gloriously refreshed, and would often
make the usual preparations for the day before glancing at
the clock to discover it was still only midnight. Feeling
completely prepared for another day, there was then nothing I could do to get to sleep again.

The Chinese doctor in charge of the hospital on the
island where I lived was a close personal friend, and he
tried everything he could think of. At last, breaking all the
rules, one morning he went in to Hongkong to see another
European friend of his, the Deputy Director of Medical
and Health Services, before whom I was summoned the
following day.

"You need a holiday," he said, before I had time to open
my mouth, "and you must get away from Hongkong."

"Perhaps," I admitted.

"Is there anywhere you could go?"

"I have a standing invitation to visit Singapore and
Sarawak."

"Could you leave in five days?"

"I suppose so, yes."

"How long would you propose going for?"

"About a fortnight?" I hazarded.

"Make it a month."

He signed a small chit, and that was that. Dazed and uncertain, I wandered into a nearby airline office, made a reservation, and sent a cable.

That night, I happened to be dining with a leading European surgeon. He expressed approval of his colleague's verdict, adding something which I found it hard to believe: that the instant I reached Singapore, I would feel perfectly normal. I left Hongkong feeling almost drunken with tiredness, and some hours later stepped out of the aircraft at Singapore, to find how mysteriously correct my surgeon friend was. All sign of fatigue had gone. As if I had never had a night of insomnia, I stayed up with friends till 3.30 a.m. and slept like a top for seven hours. Nor, in the ensuing days and weeks, was there the slightest indication of the sleepless weeks that had preceded my departure. I mention this because it is something which I still do not understand.

Shortly before leaving Hongkong, I received a personal letter from the Colonial Secretary, saying that medical opinion was that I should not return to the district, and that accordingly, at the conclusion of my holiday, I might expect to be working once more in the Secretariat. Despite the thoughtfulness that prompted the letter, I found it a bitter disappointment.

This brings out one of the strangest aspects of administrative work involving direct exposure to the people. In the Secretariat one could occasionally compliment oneself on having done a good day's work; in the district, never. All that sustained one's confidence was the hope of rectifying tomorrow the mistakes made today; and when suddenly there was not a tomorrow to count on, I found myself left facing the deplorable truth of my own inadequacy, haunted by thoughts of what I should have done, and would now never be able to do.

In these pages, the Special Magistrate will have been found lacking in numerous respects, but seldom in self-confidence. Rather the contrary: by some, his confidence of judgment may have been considered excessive, particularly when coupled with his admittedly infuriating capacity for having things his own way.

The fact is, of course, that this is the Special Magistrate's own book—as Benvenuto Cellini put it, 'written by himself'—and if he did not endeavour to make it a chronicle of his own successes, as Benvenuto did, he would be missing his opportunities.

The real truth is surely, if one comes to analyze it, that no case can ever be described as having been successfully settled, in that life permits of no perfect solutions to anything. The most one can ever hope for is to achieve agreeable settlements, in which the agreeableness can never be other than temporary, and, in fulfilment of the last of the duties of the local official, as enumerated by Hsun Ch'ing 2,200 years ago, 'urge the people to obey the government and live quietly and at ease.'

Behind that phrase lie many failures. The staff may have been right when they said that a case which did not return, after judgment had been given on it, could be counted a success. But even allowing this to be so, for every two cases harmoniously settled—for every two successes—there was one failure. It recalled Anton Tchehov's comment on life itself: that for every two paces a man takes forward, he takes one in reverse.

I must confess that the failures nearly always upset me, and curiously enough, one of the most upsetting outcomes of all occurred on my last day in the district.

In essence the problem was similar to one described earlier. It concerned an unmarried girl of about eighteen, who was with child, and who was unable to persuade the young man, who she said was the father, to admit paternity. Where it differed from the former case was in the girl herself.

Of all the uneducated girls who came to the office during my time she was incomparably the most attractive. From a village girl the most one could ever expect was a knowing look or a quickly suppressed smile, and even this but rarely. Most of them sat there stolidly, and answered questions awkwardly, being unaccustomed to speaking to a Westerner, or indeed to a government official, of whatever race. The girls from the industrial zones were in general more self-possessed, but schooled as they were by the rough and tumble of squatter life, they concealed their natures and their thoughts even more guardedly than did the country girls.

This young girl was from a town area, but she was very different from most of the others we saw. Of medium height, she had a shapely figure, lithe and well covered, and she had a charmingly springy walk. She had a round face and prominent cheeks, in which there was a very faint suggestion of red, which against her finely bronzed skin imparted a glow to her appearance, a glow which, when she spoke, was confirmed in her unusually expressive eyes. She radiated personality, happy and unspoilt.

With this, she was delightfully self-possessed. She spoke

no English, and I doubt whether she had ever before spoken to a foreigner in her life; but one would never have known it. From the moment she came into my room everything she said and did displayed complete confidence in me.

And I use the word *me* advisedly.

Chinese girls of this rare type, with a naturally engaging personality, without exception arouse suspicion in their own society, in which outward expressiveness in a woman is regarded as evidence of a moral deficiency, whether in regard to sex, or to honesty, or whatever it may be. The quality of outward reserve, which is an essential feature of Chinese good behaviour, is far more important in a woman than in a man; and the girl who is born with a naturally expressive personality lives at a permanent disadvantage.

It was interesting to watch the effect she had on the men in the office. Whatever work they might be engaged in, not one of them failed to cast a concealed glance at her; and there was not one of them, I think, to whom she did not suggest ideas. But not one of them would have trusted her. There is something in Chinese instinct which forbids trust in relation to such a girl.

I, on the contrary, instinctively trusted her, and I do not believe I was wrong. Instinct is something one develops to an acute degree in a Chinese court, where it is so exceedingly necessary. But then, of course, I was not influenced by the thousands of years which, in Chinese people, have dictated a contrary instinct.

Usually, whenever my instinct ran counter to that of members of the staff, it ultimately turned out that it was I who was wrong. This young girl provided the sole instance where, in retrospect, I would guardedly venture to say that I still believe it was I who was right, and they who were wrong. And this, may I point out, is the most presumptuous statement in this book.

The young man who, the girl claimed, had made her pregnant was a factory worker, who was probably, I would say, unsure of himself in nearly everything he did, due to the influence of his widowed mother, who displayed a degree of nastiness which even by court standards was unusual.

Seeing it from the Chinese viewpoint, one could of course sympathize with the mother. She was shocked by her son having kept company with such a girl, and appalled by the prospect of having her as a daughter-in-law.

But seen from my viewpoint, it was quite different. The mother had a possessive hold over her son, which was doing him no good; and the obstinate fury with which she conducted herself—for it was the mother's case, not the son's—and her evident hatred of the girl, which to my way of looking at it wore the appearance of an older woman's jealousy of the girl's attractiveness, drove my sympathy even more strongly towards the girl, and increased my conviction that she was telling the truth, since, in naming the young man as the father of her unborn child, she could clearly see what lay before her from her future mother-in-law.

My private judgment was that the girl would do that young man a lot of good. The standard Chinese judgment of the matter was the exact opposite.

The girl lived in a hillside hut, which she shared with her elder sister and her husband, recently married and with no children. The sister worked in a spinning factory, and the husband was a hawker. There were thus many times of day, including evenings, when one or more of them were absent; and it was contended that the younger sister, when alone in the hut, received visits from men.

At the first hearing, the widowed mother so obstructed me from questioning her son, shouting out her own answers and accusations before the boy could utter a word, that I sent them all away, telling Mr. Lo to arrange another hearing without the mother being present.

For this second hearing, the mother accompanied her son to the office and protested vigorously when she was refused admittance to see me. Consciousness of his mother's presence at the other end of the building still influenced the son, but we did get a little further. According to him, the girl had another friend; and this young fellow had been seen entering the girl's hut on the evening after the date on which she claimed to have conceived—the date on which the son himself admitted having had intercourse with her.

The friend's visit was subsequently confirmed, the other young man admitting that he had been to the girl's hut, but denying that he had ever had intercourse with her, she denying this likewise.

At this point, everything in the girl's conduct would seem to confirm the rightness of Chinese instinct in respect of her. The staff expected me to wash my hands of the matter, resigning myself to one illegitimate child the more. They could see only one reason why I persisted in seeking a solution in the girl's favour: I myself found her attractive—in which indeed they were quite right. I did.

But my instinct, contrary to theirs, told me that the girl, though she had behaved unwisely, was telling the truth. My belief was that the young man, though he would not admit it, had promised to marry her before she had allowed him to have his way of her. As a subsequent hearing with the two of them showed, he liked her, and *wanted* to believe her. But he too, being Chinese, shared the instinct of his race when it comes to a girl like this, and his mother had activated this instinct in him. With one half of his mind he was sure he was the father, with the other half unsure. Throughout every hearing, the girl remained patently and honestly sure he was.

Playing partly on his liking for the girl, and partly on his personal honour, I won his agreement to marrying her, should blood tests suggest that the child was his. Immediately after this, I called in the mother, who was, as usual, waiting to take her son home, and in the angriest scene that ever took place in my office, finally brought her to agree that, if medical science should demonstrate that the child was her son's, she must consent to his marriage.

But, this done, I found myself confronting the problem of my own ignorance. Was it possible to determine the blood group of an unborn child? Feeling rather foolish, I asked Mr. Lo, and was relieved to find that he, the father of (I believe) nine children, did not know either.

I telephoned the superintendent of Hongkong's largest hospital, to be informed that there was no other course but to wait till the baby was born, after which, if I would send the various parties concerned to the hospital, the superintendent would be happy to arrange for the necessary tests to be done. I explained this to the three of them, advising the girl to be patient and not to worry.

During the months that followed she came twice on her own to see me. She feared, perhaps, the possibility of the European officer being replaced by someone else, and her case being forgotten. Each time it gave me the same pleasure to see her.

On the second of these short visits, she thanked me for

my kindness to her—it was my duty—and lingered, as if in need of reassurance. It was a wretched position for her. I felt sure the mother was still trying to poison her son's mind against her.

"Now be sure you have no worries," I said to her gently. "When the time comes, go to the clinic and have your baby, in complete confidence that everything will turn out all right. Then, when you are ready, let me know, and the blood tests will be carried out under a government doctor's supervision."

I wished I could have told her what would most truly have reassured her—the fact that I myself believed her—but this, of course, I could not, the magistrate's word being law. But she went away smiling and a little reassured.

There followed my weeks of insomnia—not caused, I might add, by thinking about the girl, though someone did ask me whether a woman was the cause—and the order to take a holiday.

On my last day in the district I attended a meeting of the Tsuen Wan committee, at which we discussed the town's future development. The meeting had broken up, and the chairman, a highly educated man of great understanding, was escorting me to my car when it occurred to me that at about this time the pretty girl's child would be due. I asked the chairman if he knew of the case.

He did—and also, I suspect, of the staff's views concerning my particular interest in it. Laughing, as Chinese so often do when imparting news they know will hurt, he told me what had happened.

Only two days previously she had died giving birth to a stillborn child.

I stopped in my stride, and in front of the whole committee, I covered my face with my hands. I could see the girl then as she was at the last instant I set eyes on her, when at the doorway departing, on a sudden impulse she had turned back to me, and with a little smile, said:

"You won't forget me, will you?"

Indeed, I never will. I could have wept when they told me. Irrational as it may seem, I felt at that moment personally responsible for her death; and whenever I think of her, even now, the same feelings return. The news was the knife-thrust which human affairs always deliver in the end.

Nor perhaps, when one comes to think of it, was it so irrational, after all, to feel responsible. Rather, perhaps, could it be said to be natural in one who has been called upon to assume the strange responsibilities of being 'the father and mother of the people'.

I had often wondered what the staff really thought of me. It was vanity, I conceded, to ask such questions of myself; and since there would be twenty different answers, none of which were ever likely to reach me, I had long been resigned to never knowing. Nevertheless, in the somewhat unusual circumstances of being the only European in charge of (as it then was) an entirely Oriental staff, it was a question which inevitably recurred, whenever I omitted to tell vanity to keep quiet.

In the car, being driven back to Kowloon, Mr. Lo, the bastion of the staff's own conservatism and reticence with me, gave me a surprise, which mitigated somewhat the wretchedness in which I had been plunged by the news of the young girl's death—wretchedness amid which I was mentally searching for the overlooking point which, recognized, might have caused matters to have ended other than as they had.

Seated side by side in the rear seat, we were discussing

the years that had passed since the day when I first walked into the office and read with consternation the Governor's mandate, when Mr. Lo, gazing out of the window at the passing hills, said reflectively, "Well, this I can say. I've never had to work so hard in my life as during these years. But I've never enjoyed it so much."

It is a compliment which I shall never forget, and which I should be ashamed of myself for recording. But, as I said just now, this is the Special Magistrate's own book, and to any who may find it annoying that he should include praise of himself, may I pass the reminder that it was the Special Magistrate's personal technique to annoy people. The indulgent reader will, I hope, have shared my desire to know the answer to this question, and will have appreciated that it was only one of the answers. What the remaining nineteen were, no one knows.

Early next morning, one of my Secretariat colleagues telephoned me at my town apartment to remind me to be sure, before departing, to return my instrument.

As restrainedly and circumspectly as possible, I inquired of him what particular instrument of mine it could be which he felt in need of.

With a certain *soulagement*, I learned that he was referring merely to a piece of paper—the frightening document on the basis of which it all began. This document, it transpired, had to be returned to the Secretariat for cancellation.

"Could I please have it back after it's been cancelled?" I inquired.

"Have it back?" an incomprehending voice demanded. "What for?"

Reduced by his authoritative tone—I had forgotten how

awful we all were in the Secretariat—to the timidity of a mouse, I said meekly:

"I—er—thought it would be rather nice to have as a souvenir."

"H'm. Odd sort of souvenir," came the reply.

"But still, could I have it?"—you know the Special Magistrate by this time.

"Well, I suppose so. If you *want* it," he said with lordly indifference.

" 'Less than the dust beneath thy chariot-wheel'," I murmured to myself as I put the phone down, and a moment later found myself marvelling at the curious fact that I should have devoted so many years to trying to understand other people, when I seemed to know so little about my own. To how many Westerners in this world is it given to be a *Chinese* magistrate? But I believe that fellow would have consented to lose his own instrument rather than agree with me.

Kai Tak Airport being on the Kowloon side of the harbour, the true Hongkong Islander sets forth on his travels in a manner which classes him at once among the world's super-exclusive. The tourist can be recognized by the cameras and odd little bags which dangle around him. The experienced traveller can be denoted by the minimal luggage he carries. The super-exclusive cannot be detected, since they carry nothing.

Luggage having been sent cross-harbour to the airport by invisible agency, the true Hongkong Islander leaves his apartment, closes the door, strolls down to the ferry, pays 10 cents, and crosses to Kowloon, giving no indication that his purpose in doing so is anything other than to purchase a roll of silk or a tea tray.

On this particular occasion, my successor—a brilliant young Chinese who, the reader will learn with relief, had passed his law examination—had sent the office car for me. A signature was required of me at the office. The Special Magistrate, it appeared—and as would surely seem proper—was the only one who could sign away his own instrument.

It was a fine, hot, summer afternoon, and at the office a horrendous one. The whole world seemed to have come in for one thing or another. The place was packed with people.

Staff and members of the public acknowledged me as I came in, but everyone was too busy to do more than that. With a sense of bereftness, I observed how busily the busy district revolved, even though it no longer revolved around me. Personal rule has this in its nature, that the discovery that, as a person, one was not intrinsically necessary to it—that many others would have done the same, and better—is disheartening in the way it reduces one to size in the end. Edging my way past the people in the passage, I felt like a ghost in a roomful of living people. Mine was no longer a voice they would hear.

At what had once been my desk, I found my successor tensely absorbed in work, unable to give more than a few seconds to any interruption, his appearance foreshadowing what I had often felt to be needed, and what the government in due course decided on—the division of the district into two, creating a fourth district, with double the staff in both.

I signed the letter, returning the mandate that had once so startled me—even the renewed sight of it made me feel uncomfortable—wished my successor well, and passing the outer offices for the last time, in descending order of exaltation, and with no one with any time to say goodbye to me, was driven to the airport.

The aircraft took off in the direction of the sea, and having a seat on the port side, the whole of the eastern part of the district lay for a few precious minutes beneath me.

Green and hilly, with its indented valleys, its complicated inlets, its islands and stark headlands defying the smooth but deceptive China Sea, the district looked exactly the same as when I last saw it from the air, on returning from leave to take up my appointment. The administration, it seemed, in my time, had made no visible effect on it whatever.

And then I remembered something. Scanning one of the more remote but fertile valleys, I detected a minute white spot. It was so small that only the forewarned eye would have found it.

It was a bridge, sturdily built in concrete and stone, across a river which flooded seasonally; and its main purpose was to enable children from three or four villages on one side of the river to reach their school, which was on the other side. It had been erected under the direction of a committee of elders from all the villages concerned, with financial and other material assistance from the administration.

In the Chinese countryside, to build a bridge or a road is an act of virtue. Built into the side of that bridge, where wayfarers might see it, was a large slab of white granite, on which was engraved the date of the bridge's construction and a brief account of the circumstances, followed by the names of all those who had subscribed to the cost of it, or otherwise materially assisted.

The stone itself was of the most durable; and in that it gave the names of all the local notables of the day, it constituted a historical record, which the villagers would not wish to lose. Even should the bridge one day be replaced by something larger, the stone with its inscription would be preserved. It might, for example, be inserted into a wall of the temple.

Heading the list of names on that stone was my own, with my style and title.

The outlying islands and rocks receded, the aircraft heading south, mounting over the sunlit emptiness of the China Sea. And then something else occurred to me.

My name on that inscription beside the bridge was, of course, my Chinese name—Kao Tze—and although, being a very apposite name, it might suggest that there had once been an officer in the district who for some reason used a pen-name, it gave absolutely no indication whatever that the officer was not Chinese, while the title of office was that of an imperial mandarin.

That inscription was my sole memorial, and not even on that could it be recorded that I was a European, since this would have been improper. Throughout the district, all trace of me as a Westerner would not exactly be obliterated; it would be treated as a fact which did not exist. Similarly, when China adopts or utilizes anything from another civilization, that thing becomes Chinese in the process, and any indication that it is of foreign origin will vanish, like drawings on sand before an incoming tide.

For a Westerner—or for the West—to believe it is possible in any way to influence China is chimerical. When a Westerner comes to China, no matter how high his rank or how great his influence, all that he can achieve—all that he will ever achieve—is to add a grain of salt to sea-water, since China, like the sea, is adamantine, and of unchanging substance.

Yet, as I settled myself more comfortably in my seat, and thought of the crabs I had been promised for midnight supper with Chinese friends in Singapore, I already knew that, speaking for myself, and despite all it might suggest of thanklessness to be utterly forgotten in that district, it would always be a pleasure, from out of that void, to recall and relate a strange truth.

As the engraved stone beside that bridge will for long years confirm, I was once myself a mandarin.